Women and Men in Late Eighteenth-Century Egypt

Modern Middle East Series, No. 18
Sponsored by the Center for Middle Eastern Studies
The University of Texas at Austin

Women and Men in Late Eighteenth-Century Egypt

Afaf Lutfi al-Sayyid Marsot

UNIVERSITY OF TEXAS PRESS
AUSTIN

Requests for permission to reproduce material from this work should be sent
to Permissions, University of Texas Press, Box 7819, Austin, TX 78713-7819.

∞ The paper used in this publication meets the minimum requirements of
American National Standard for Information Sciences—Permanence of Paper
for Printed Library Materials, ANSI Z39.48-1984.

Library of Congress Cataloging-in-Publication Data

Sayyid-Marsot, Afaf Lutfi.
Women and men in late eighteenth-century Egypt /
Afaf Lutfi al-Sayyid Marsot. — 1st ed.
p.   cm. —(Modern Middle East series ; 18) Includes bibliographical
references (p.   ) and index. ISBN 0-292-71736-9   (alk. paper : cloth)
1. Social classes—Egypt—History—18th century.   2. Women—Egypt—
History—18th century.   3. Sex role—Egypt—History—18th century.
4. Women—Egypt—Economic conditions.   5. Elite (Social sciences)—
Egypt—History—18th century.   I. Title.   II. Series: Modern Middle
East series (Austin, Tex.) ; 18.
HN786.Z9S674   1995
305.3'0962'09033—dc20   95-17236

To the memory of Elizabeth Monroe

and

to Vanina and Vanessa

CONTENTS

PREFACE

The impetus for this book came from reading André Raymond's superb two-volume work dealing with the eighteenth century, *Artisans et commerçants au Caire au XVIIIème siècle*. His work did not deal with women, which is why I decided to research that topic. I hope this book will inspire researchers to delve deeper into the archives dealing with women in that period and eventually bring to light the full picture of women's participation in the economy in different Muslim countries. I therefore consider this a preliminary essay, which sketches some main themes and is certainly not the definitive work on the subject.

Two colleagues in Egypt helped with the research: Dr. Mustafa Muhammad Ramadan of al-Azhar University and Dr. A. Afifi of Cairo University. Dr. Ramadan, at my request, researched the citadel archives for copies of deeds made out by mostly elite women. Dr. Afifi looked into the Qisma archives for similar deeds and also for probate records, while I looked into the *awqaf* archives in the Shahr Al-aqari. Some of these records duplicate one another since all property is cited in probate records.

The research on this book was carried out through a generous grant from the Joint Committee of the Near and Middle East of the Social Science Research Council, to which I am most grateful.

I am also grateful to Drs. R. Abu-l Haj, Terry Walz, and Nancy Gallagher and to Christine Ahmed and Sherry Vatter, who generously read versions of the manuscript and helped improve it. I am especially grateful to Dr. Nelly Hanna and Dr. M. A. Serag, whose help has been invaluable. I am equally grateful to my husband, Dr. Alain Marsot, who patiently listened to me, advised me, and allowed me to monopolize the computer. Last, but not least, I owe a debt to my two daughters, Vanina and Vanessa Marsot, who edited parts of the work and helped tighten the argument. Any errors in the book are of course my own responsibility. To all of the above I owe more than words can express.

INTRODUCTION

During the reign of Muhammad Ali legal documents were collected from the various courts and deposited in one area. Since then the documents have been moved to various places, finally ending up at the Registry Office, the Shahr al-Aqari, in 1970.

Another set of deeds pertaining to the Ottoman period, dealing with financial and commercial transactions and with litigation, was preserved in the National Archives (Dar al-Wathaiq) in the citadel in 1971 (they have now been moved to a new repository on the Nile at Imbaba). These are of two kinds. Deeds pertaining to sultans and amirs are placed in cartons (*mahfadha*) and numbered from 1 to 364. Deeds pertaining to ordinary people are preserved in folders numbered 1 to 4,978.

The folders I used began with no. 7, dated 1184/1770 to 1190/1776, which held 80 deeds, of which 33 pertained to women. The contents of this carton were numbered 301–380. Chronological order is not always followed: some deeds in no. 7 are dated 1190/1776, while other deeds in no. 8 are dated 1186/1772. The numbers of the cartons have been changed since André Raymond, author of the two-volume work entitled *Artisans et commerçants au Caire au XVIIIème siècle*,[1] the first to use these archives, consulted them over two decades ago, so that his carton no. 5 is our carton no. 10.

Carton no. 8, dated 1186/1772–1194/1780, was numbered 380–420; it contained 41 deeds, 15 pertaining to women. No. 9, dated 1174/1760–1196/1781, was numbered 421–472; this had 51 deeds, of which 12 pertained to women. No. 10 had 85 deeds, dated 1172/1758–1199/1784 and numbered 453–537, including 21 for women. No. 15, dated 1210/1795–1227/1812 and numbered 686–733, had 48 deeds, 16 for women. No. 16, dated 1212/1797 and numbered 734–779, had 46 deeds, out of

1

which 22 belonged to women. Of the 351 deeds I consulted, 119 or 34 percent of the total belonged to women.

All of these deeds pertain to the exchange of property: to loans, buying and selling, mortmain endowments, or trust funds known as *awqaf* (sing. *waqf*, also *waqfiyya* and pl. *waqfiyyat* or *awqaf*). In brief they reveal the personal and financial relations of individuals, for any transaction must be registered in the court to render it valid and binding.

Other than the deeds in the citadel we have a second lot of deeds from two courts entitled "military division" (Qisma Askariyya) and "Arab division" (Qisma Arabiyya). These are court registers which list estates of deceased individuals in order to levy an inheritance tax collected by the regiments. Individuals who were related in some fashion to the Ottoman regiments (relatives, retainers, supporters, etc.) were listed under the Qisma Askariyya, while the rest went under the Qisma Arabiyya. In the early part of the eighteenth century most of the estates pertained to the Qisma Askariyya, since artisans and *ocaqs* (Ottoman regiments) had a symbiotic relationship, with the *ocaqs* protecting the artisans in return for a fee. After the middle of the century the relationship diminished as the *ocaqs* lost their influence. Those who were registered in the Qisma Askariyya then came to have little or no connection with the *ocaqs*. Raymond believes that the Qisma Askariyya concerned the estates of Muslims, while the Qisma Arabiyya showed a preponderance of non-Muslim or *dhimmi* estates. I have found an occasional *dhimmi* in the Qisma Askariyya, although most were registered in the Qisma Arabiyya; I also found that in the period from 1166/1752 to 1201/1786 there were a majority of Muslims in the Qisma Arabiyya.

Thus while the deeds in the citadel indicate transactions involving various kinds of properties which have been bought or sold (without necessarily telling us when the owner died and how many of these properties remained in the owner's possession), the deeds of the Qisma give details of items in an estate on which an inheritance tax would be levied.

The third lot of deeds we possess, which may or may not duplicate the deeds in either the citadel or the Qisma, are straightforward trust deeds (*awqaf*) or endowed properties in mortmain. These are of two kinds. The *waqf khairi* deed property in perpetuity for a charitable cause, such as prayers to be recited at certain times, the upkeep and maintenance of a school, or the support of the blind and the widowed. The manager of any trust (the *nazir*) was a male or female family member, a respectable individual, or often an *alim* (pl. ulama). Prominent ulama were managers of many *awqaf*, which supplied them with wealth and hence power. Shaikh al-Sadat, the head of a mystical order and one of the most powerful religious figures of his day, supervised some fifty-two *awqaf*.

The second kind of *waqf* was the *waqf ahli*, set up in favor of the donor then after the donor's death in favor of family members and their descendants. There was always a clause which included some charity in the *waqf*; the law would not recognize a *waqf* without some endowment for charitable purposes stipulated in the contents. These charities might be immediate, such as prayers recited at specific times of the year or food distributed to the poor, or ultimate, such as after the deaths of all descendants of the donor. When the donors had no descendants the *waqf* was frequently in favor of manumitted mamluks (*maatiq*) and their descendants. When all persons related to the donor had died then the *waqf* would sustain a chosen charity. Only the revenues from the *waqf* were disbursed; the capital remained untouched.

These deeds give us some details about women's commercial and financial transactions and the kinds of property in which they invested. They also supply certain details about gender relations: for example, a husband borrowing money from his wife and registering it in a legal deed or remitting such funds a few years later in the form of a piece of property or the widow of a mamluk who remarried and fictitiously or actually sold her husband some property.

The above material (nearly eight hundred documents) forms the crux of this book, supplemented by anecdotes from Abd al-Rahman al-Jabarti, our leading historical source for the period, and others that reveal much about the mamluk and indigenous society of the country.

Some terms need explanations:
barrani: a tax added to the land tax (*miri*) levied by the Ottoman government.
faiz: the amount left over after the legal taxes were remitted to the administration by the tax-farmer (*multazim*), which constituted his or her profit.

hanut: a shop.

hasil: a depot or storage room.

hikr: ground rent on *waqf* property.

hiyaza: land tenure.

hush (the dialect pronunciation) or *hawsh*: a large area in which small huts were built for urban slum dwellings; also a courtyard within a house.

isqat haqq: renunciation of rights to a portion or the entirety of a *waqf*.

istibdal: a form of exchange whereby a *waqf* property is sold and replaced by another equivalent property that becomes a *waqf* in its place.

makan: a place of habitation or building, which may house workshops (*qaas*) with weaving looms and shops, some with stories above (*tabaqas*) for rental or storage (see Appendices A to C).

maqaad: part of a house.

muakhar sadaqa: the back dowry, that is, the balance of the dowry due registered in a marriage contract and paid on divorce or death.

mudaf: a tax added to the *miri* tax.

qaa: workshop, usually containing weaving looms; also a hallway in a house.

rab: tenement.

riwaq: area in a *wikala*, somewhat akin to a shopping center today; also the term used for student dormitories in al-Azhar, much like a college in an English university.

tasarruf: use.

wikala: a *khan* or area with shops, storehouses, and dwellings where merchants could store their wares, buy and sell their goods, and find rooms for lodging.

coinage: the common coin was the *para*, also known as *nisf fidda* and *medin*. This was the smallest denomination. The *para* was worth 90 *riyals* (the *riyal* was a fictional coin not actually minted). The larger coins in circulation were the Spanish *piastre*, the Austrian *Thaler*, and the Ottoman *kis* (purse), equal to 500 *paras*.[2]

1

WOMEN IN THE EYES OF MEN
Myth and Reality

Much of the history of Egypt has been written from the focal point of men. In the rare instances when women were mentioned, they were treated as little more than appendages to famous men or discussed within abstract theoretical concepts produced by Muslim legists, dating from the eighth and ninth centuries. These works, written from a strictly male point of view, defined what women were, how they should behave, and what their position in a male-dominated society was to be. Consequently myths and legends arose in literature regarding proper norms of behavior for women, derogating them and sustaining the image of women's sexuality as presenting a potential danger to men. Hence the need to keep them segregated and secluded from male company, rendering them "invisible" in the words of some anthropologists. The home came to be regarded as the domain of women and the marketplace—outside the home and, significantly, the arena where wealth is generated—that of men. At least that was the image which the male establishment projected as reality.

Some scholars believe that women are subordinate in all societies, sexual inequality being a societal fundamental. Others believe male dominance to be the outcome of "control over production and distribution of valued goods and wealth."[1] Jack Goody, for example, has found that a dominant role for men developed in societies with advanced agricultural means such as the plow. In societies that used the hoe there was greater equality among the sexes and even a dominant role for women.[2] Still others point out that dominance has variable meanings: it is possible for women to be subordinate in some spheres and dominant in others—that is, "visible" in some spheres and "invisible" in others.

The activities of women in any given society are dependent on a wealth of political and economic determinants. Religious and social determinants may sustain and encourage changes due to economic factors, although it is more likely that all the determinants are intertwined in a complex relationship.

Islam came to a society that was made up of urban merchants, but also of agriculturalists, for the oasis of Medina, to which the Prophet emigrated when he left Mecca, was agricultural. Later the Muslims expanded into other agricultural societies, such as Egypt, Syria, and Iraq, where the plow had long been in use. It may well be that the paternalistic framework was set in these societies, as Goody supposes. The characteristics of the system were the control of men over women and their domination over the sources of wealth.

In varying degrees, which differed from tribe to tribe in Arabia and from country to country, the customs and mores of these countries were often incorporated into Islamic law, the *sharia.* Furthermore, specific historical circumstances pushed various political entities toward developing their own habits. While Muslims pride themselves on forming a Muslim community (the *umma* or unity of believers), they accept different customs, an outgrowth of historical realities. The Prophet said, "Difference of opinion in my community is a blessing." That helps explain why four schools of orthodox Sunni jurisprudence arose in various parts of the new Muslim empire, so that there is no one homogeneous whole.

Consequently we must expect to find different attitudes toward women arising at various historical epochs in a Muslim civilization that reached from the Atlantic to the Pacific for over fourteen centuries. Gender relations are determined by politics, religion, culture, changes in the modes of production, and changes in the environment. It is the interplay of these determinants that modifies gender relations at any given time. While the theoretical condition of women was interpreted in a certain fashion during one historical period, that condition actually changed at other times and under other circumstances. Such changes can clearly be noted when the activities of women during different historical periods are compared, as during the eighteenth and the nineteenth centuries in Egypt.

The static image of gender relations in which women were subordinated, exploited, and shoved into the social background, while true to a degree for some sectors of society, is belied in some historical periods such as the last half of the eighteenth century in Egypt. During this period women played an active role in the marketplace, corroborating the assumption that they played a more active role in other sectors of society and during other periods. That role generally has been neglected by male historians; hence the need for a social history with the accent as much on women as on men in order to balance the bias of male-dominated accounts and to present missing insights. It is true that it is more difficult to write such a history since archives and chronicles seldom mention women, except for legal records which give accounts of litigation between members of both sexes or lists of endowments, successions, and property records. For example, 30 to 40 percent of deeds registered in the last half of the eighteenth century were made out by women, yet few authors have thought to examine them. Why have women been ignored?

Recent works by social historians that have asked questions regarding women, not only in Egypt but elsewhere in the region, have always found evidence of the important economic role of women. Ronald Jennings, Abraham Marcus, and others writing on women in various regions of the Ottoman Empire such as Kayseri or Syria have come up with evidence that women were certainly active partners in their societies and not the passive, "invisible" beings that past authors had led us to expect.

Yet if we look closely at historical works of the past, such as Abd al-Rahman al-Jabarti's chronicle of events in the eighteenth century and the first decades of the nineteenth century or Nicolas Turc's account of the French occupation of Egypt or the Damurdash Chronicles, which re-counted conflicts between military units, we find a certain amount of anecdotal material dealing with women that has been overlooked. If we examine collections of *fatwas* (legal opinions given by muftis or jurisconsults), as Judith Tucker did in her work on nineteenth-century women in Egypt, we find legal opinions delivered in response to many concrete cases of litigation involving women. We discover that women managed large estates, sued in court, and generally involved themselves in the marketplace—using the term loosely to mean the economic and mercantile life of their times.

When this anecdotal or legal information is supplemented by archival information from endowment trust deeds or court registers of transactions, we find that a different social image of both genders appears. Far from being a stagnant society where the rulers ruled and the population suffered in silence—where women were mere chattel—Egypt at this time was a dynamic society characterized by change and turmoil, in which women certainly played an important part.

This work aims to present a picture of late eighteenth-century society, showing the roles that both men and women played in different social strata. The following chapter examines the political struggles that pitted mamluk households against one another and helped women develop a greater degree of participation in economic affairs than heretofore.

The third chapter deals with the mamluk and Ottoman elites and the fourth with the native elites, the ulama and *tujjar* (merchants), showing the access to sources of wealth of the women of such strata. Women's investments and access to wealth indicate that the market was fairly open to investors of both sexes, without differentiation between them. Wealth indicates a modicum of power. It is difficult for me to believe that a wealthy woman had no power in her society, no matter how closed that society may have been. Nafisa Khatun and her ilk are a case in point. Wealthy women had choices and were not as dependent as poor women on the whims of a male, especially when the woman controlled her wealth herself (and it is clear that many women of that period did control their wealth). They also relied on the ulama to see that justice was done and had no compunction about going to court and suing to obtain such rights—a situation in clear contrast with the later nineteenth century.

The fifth chapter concentrates on the artisanal groups, while the final chapter is a comparison between the situation of women in the eighteenth century (when society took on certain characteristics as the result of a decentralized form of government and a series of natural disasters and foreign occupations) and the nineteenth century (when government was centralized, leading to social changes that undermined the position of women and marginalized them).

Part of women's ability to participate actively in matters of an economic nature was due to interpretations of Islamic religious injunctions by male scholars. Thus, while these interpretations allowed women an economic role, they also included limitations on their freedom to maneuver.

The role generally ascribed to women by Muslim ulama is usually expressed in two ways. First, whatever is written regarding women in the Quran is immutable. Second, ulama have interpreted passages in the Quran in certain ways according to the exigencies of the day.

The Quran states that humanity was created in pairs (*zawj*), who have the same religious obligations and duties. Both are doers—workers—and their functions are recognized: "I never neglect to recompense any worker [*amilin*] among you, male or female, you are equal to each other."[3]

Women, like men, inherit from paternal and maternal relations, siblings, and offspring, but where a male inherits a whole part the woman inherits half that portion. The wisdom behind this is that a woman's property is hers to do with as she pleases, while a man is enjoined to support the family; thus his is the heavier financial burden. When the companions of the Prophet learned this, they were outraged and wondered why women should inherit at all if they were to be totally supported by men.[4] Another passage in the Quran specifies that men support women: "Men are caretakers of women since God favored some of them over others and because they spend of their wealth" ("al-rijal qawwamun ala-l nisa bima faddala allahu badahum ala badin wa bima anfaqu min amwalihim").[5] This passage has been subject to different interpretations. Men have often interpreted it to mean that men are "guardians" or "overseers" (*qawwamun*) over women, since they are "favored" (*faddala Allahu badahum* [men] *ala badin* [women], a relationship in which the man is superior to the woman). Some men and women have interpreted the passage simply to mean that men are the protectors of women in the physical sense because God has favored (*faddala*) them with greater strength and that they are also materially responsible for them.

While a sense of responsibility may or may not imply a power relationship of superior to inferior, this passage confirmed the male sense of dominance and was one element that sustained a paternalistic relationship within a marriage. It was not the only element. Other passages in the Quran grant a woman half a man's portion, specify that two female witnesses are needed in order to testify in court (where only one male is necessary), and allow men to repudiate women while women have to sue for divorce. These have all added fuel to notions of male supremacy. Islam changed gender relationships as they existed in the pre-Islamic period, which varied in different tribes, and instituted a universal system of legal rights. Muslims, especially Muslim males, tried to change that by reinterpreting the system to give them supremacy. But if both spouses are two halves of a whole (*zawj*) in religious terms, wherein lies the supremacy? It lies in the economic, political, and social fields. In the past it was assumed that women played no part in the economic field since they were not merchants or involved in commerce. Today we learn that women were indeed involved in the economic field as investors and consumers and as holders of property. It is in the political and legal fields that women were "invisible," at least publicly so, for we know from various accounts how women at different times in history did play a powerful political role as the wives or mothers of rulers, as we shall see.

If men are "caretakers" over women, then the next step is to treat women as minors, unable to make decisions on their own. This is sustained by *hadiths* (sayings of the Prophet, many invented) stating that women lack brains and religion (*naqisat aql wa din*). In reality, the Prophet had respect for women and engaged in discussions with them, taking care to clarify points of religion. In his day women attended public meetings and were an intrinsic part of the marketplace. The best examples are Khadija, the Prophet's wife, employer, and the one with wealth; and Hind, the wife of Abu Sufyan, the foremost long-distance merchant of the day. Many sayings attributed to the Prophet were devised after his death. Even authentic sayings were interpreted by men who, while well intentioned, were products of their time.

Works by Fatma Mernissi, Barbara Stowasser, Jane Smith, and Leila Ahmad have supplied us with a lot more concrete information on women.[6] Stowasser's research on the early days of Islam and Mernissi's work on the Prophet's relationship with his wives have shown how active a role women had. That role was certainly more nuanced than we had been led to believe. In an oft-cited anecdote Ali admitted that a woman who corrected him on a point of law in public was right and he was wrong. In one *hadith* the Prophet enjoined Muslims to take half their religion "from the red-headed or red-cheeked [woman]," referring to Aisha, his wife. Leila Ahmad's work, while not pleasing to historians since it compresses several centuries into one whole, reinterprets nineteenth-century attitudes toward women in a more controversial fashion. The important fact about these works is that they have shown the active participation of women in society and the biases that male notions of women have created, leading us, erroneously, to assume the total subordination of women to men.

Complete control over women could not occur if they, like men, could inherit property and manage it, thus competing with men in the market-place, the arena of wealth and power. To prevent such competition it was necessary to remove the presence of women from the marketplace. This was made easy by the practice of veiling and segregation which came into vogue in the Abbassi period, especially during the reign of Harun al-Rashid (170–193/786–809). In imitation of Sassanian and Byzantine practices, the rulers segregated the women in harems guarded by eunuchs and veiled them from public view. This practice could only take place among the elites, who could afford to segregate women and buy eunuchs to guard them and servants to serve them. The rest of the population was neither segregated nor veiled.

The second source after the Quran that specified the role of women within a Muslim society were the teachings and the interpretations of the Quran made by learned men, the ulama. While there were always learned women, who were referred to as *alimat* (sing. *alima*), no woman ever acquired the status and degree of authority of a male *alim*; thus all interpretations of the Quran or the hadiths have been made by men, even when women were among the major transmitters of *hadith* s. It is men from the eighth century onward who interpreted the passage in the Quran which enjoins men and women to dress modestly to mean that women should be totally covered and segregated, neither seen nor heard. The passage in the Quran which tells women to use the head covering (*khimar*) to cover their cleavage has been interpreted as a total covering of the body. This interpretation was sustained by the Quranic passage enjoining Muslim men to talk to the wives of the Prophet from behind a veil,[7] which was interpreted by Abbassi ulama to apply to all women. The passages that mentioned the equality of men and women and those that entitled women to work were overlooked in favor of passages that were interpreted to mean a lesser role for women in order to reinforce a paternalistic system.

With the advent of asceticism and mysticism, which stressed renun-ciation of the body in favor of the spirit, female sexuality became an issue. Islam regards marriage as a duty and frowns on monasticism, so mystics could not prohibit marriage; instead they regarded female sexuality as a trap for men, leading them to forget their religious duties. Women, they asserted, should be segregated and kept ignorant lest they learn of their sexual powers and lead men to sin. Ghazali (died 505/1111), a famous teacher, believed that the whole of woman was a blemish (*awra*). Her sexuality was so strong that even one look was enough to weaken a man and thus she had to be kept hidden away from the eyes of men lest she lead them into temptation. None of this has any basis in the Quran, which stresses the equality of both genders.

One must insert a note of caution here that the veil meant different things at different times. It could mean total covering of the face and body, covering the hair only (which is culture specific and applies equally to both sexes), or, as in modern days, a variety of degrees of modesty in female garb.

Yet in spite of segregation and veiling, Harun al-Rashid's mother, his cousin/wife Zubaida, and his sisters were powerful women. Al-Hadi, Harun's brother and predecessor on the throne, was so incensed at his mother's constant exercising of authority in affairs of state, which she had also done during his father's reign, that he forbade men from seeking audience with her. The wife, mother, or sister of any ruler could wield influence through her closeness to him and her ability to manipulate him. Indeed women's intercession was frequently sought by the powerful of the day. Men of various walks of life had access to the caliph's mother—hence the ruler's prohibition against appealing to her.[8] This begs the question of how strict segregation was then. The same powerful position was attributed to Zubaida and to the ruler's sisters, who could get powerful men removed from office, engaged in wheeling and dealing in the marketplace, and were fabulously wealthy women.[9]

During later periods when wealth was not as plentiful or when the ruler was not as accommodating, women played a more retiring role. In the Ottoman age there was a period referred to by historiographers as the age of women or Sultanate of Women, in which mothers of sultans (valide sultans) were the real rulers. When the man on the throne had been incarcerated in a "golden cage," a palace, from puberty until he came to the throne, with only women and eunuchs for companions, women and eunuchs played a powerful role in affairs of state. It was valide sultans who saved the empire when they called the Köprülüs to power during the reign of a ruler best remembered for fathering over 140 children, leaving little time for affairs of state.[10]

Throughout the reigns of sultans, competent or otherwise, mothers played a powerful role. Indeed, in all Muslim families mothers play an important role, not least because the Prophet said, "Heaven lies at the feet of mothers." Since women have the primary function of child rearing, they have the greatest influence on their sons. It did not require a Sigmund Freud to teach women that a mother who indoctrinated a son until the age of puberty would remain the most powerful focus in his eyes. The paternalistic system granted mothers status through their male children, so women as well as men helped perpetuate that system.

A paternalistic system is aided and reinforced by a centralized form of power or by a hierarchic form of government, where sources of wealth are distributed by the ruler and his supporters, as during the Ottoman age. Yet throughout history we can see that women, in spite of being second-class citizens, were able to endow charities and become involved in financial activities, including trade and commerce and other income-generating activities. Even during the most paternalistic eras women were able to participate in economic activities through the Quranic right of inherit- ance. As noted, the Quran specified that women were to inherit one-half a male's share. Wives inherited one-eighth or one-fourth if there were no children, while sisters and brothers (uterine, full, and agnate) or the nearest male heirs inherited the rest of the estate.

Muslims could only disinherit legal heirs by going through a convo- luted process. They could get around the laws of inheritance by deeding property in a will, but only one-third the total property could be willed; the rest had to be legally inherited. A parent who tried to cut out legal heirs by selling all the property and spending the money on frivolous living (*safah*) could be sued by the heirs in court for wasting their patrimony. The court would put the parent under trusteeship, disburse living expenses, and invest the remainder until the wasted wealth had been accumulated once more. One could buy property and register it in another person's name, however, such as buying a house and registering it in the wife's name, thereby cutting out children from an earlier marriage.

Setting up a trust fund, a mortmain endowment, was a means of preventing the patrimony from being wasted and also of favoring whichever heirs one wished. Endowed property, in theory, could be neither sold nor mortgaged, though ways were invented for getting around that. A trust or *waqf* could consist of the entirety of an estate and could cut out legal heirs or redistribute property to those whom the donor chose (e.g., males but not females).

The degree of economic involvement of women differed from one historical period to another. At times when the government was loosely controlled by the rulers or when government was decentralized women had greater opportunities for money making. I shall try to show that this happened during the second half of the eighteenth century.

Being involved in the marketplace also has a political implication. The fact that women were not appointed to public or legal office did not mean that they were devoid of political influence. Women could use other methods to wield influence indirectly: "manipulation, maneuvering, bluff, gossip, nagging . . . are important components of political activity often neglected in earlier studies."[11] These informal strategies of political participation were effective, for women had access to male elites, if only in the privacy of the bedroom. Although one cannot measure such influence, it would be a mistake to overlook it.

Furthermore, women had great social influence. They were the guardians of tradition, the purveyors of social wisdom, the teachers of etiquette and manners—the ones who set the standards and the tone for any society through teaching the younger generations. But just as women manipulated men, so men manipulated women. When men needed women's participation, learned men began to give differing interpretations of the role of women—such as pointing out that investments were legitimate for all Muslims and profit was good, as happened during the eighteenth century.

I have mentioned the economic factor as playing a part in gender differentiation within a society. Modern sociologists offer a further determinant that helps explain relationships between the sexes. Education in past ages was limited to a small proportion of society. The larger mass of both sexes was illiterate. Among the elites both men and women were literate in religion and in language, the Quran being the best teacher of Arabic grammar. Thus a hierarchy based on education only existed in the sense that ulama and alimat were more educated than any other sector of society. Many works of different historical ages mention learned women, stating that a woman studied with her father or with his colleagues and giving names of her teachers.[12] Learned women generally came from families of ulama, although no one has yet made a quantitative study of these women comparing them with their male counterparts.

Among the mamluks neither sex was literate when they came to Egypt. Both had to be taught religion and converted (thus made partially literate) and taught a common language. Here again education was not different among the sexes. Parity then existed between mamluk men and women in the sense that both became conversant with the principles of Arabic in order to perform their religious duties. Some even became learned men and women. The rest were content to defer to paid employees. Each mamluk household had a number of scribes, accountants, and clerks who filled the gap (if it existed) in the administration and management of property for either sex. The same kind of education or lack of education, when allied to a higher death rate among men than women, would tend to minimize patriarchy and to enhance the role of women. Men normally married women who were much younger, but the higher death rate among men negated the difference in years, which tended to give men an edge over women. Mamluk men may have married women who were older than they were, for they married women for their socioeconomic position rather than women who pleased them sexually—these they bought. This is characteristic of late eighteenth-century mamluk society.

A further determinant in that society was the erosion of the power of the state as a consequence of the mamluks' inability, save sporadically, to establish a strong centralized government. The erosion of centralized power led inexorably to the creation of collaborative linkages among the members of society. The ulama acquired a greater degree of power,[13] as did the Sufi orders and indeed the artisanal guilds. This is exemplified by the frequency of riots and disturbances involving ulama and guild members that characterized that period. In such times when the patriarchy is generally weakened the role of women strengthens. Thus women's role was greater in both social and economic terms at times when (1) the degree of education among the sexes was not greatly different, in that both were not highly educated (with the exception of the strata of ulama), (2) the patriarchal centralized system of government was weakened, (3) the life span of males was short because of conditions of violence and infighting, and (4) the difference in age between the spouses was not large and the woman was sometimes older than the male.[14] It might then be possible to say that in such a society men amass wealth, but women invest and control it. A certain unwritten contract may even have existed between married couples, in which the woman was the paramount authority within the household and the man was the paramount authority outside the household.

It is by now a truism that women do not have as much freedom to maneuver in a politically stable patriarchal system as they would in a more fluid system, when new opportunities for financial activities present themselves and the patriarchal stranglehold on the economy is in consequence loosened. One expects changes during periods of crisis and instability. Such changes may lead to different investments or to new investors in the market. Among these investors were women. The political turmoil that swept over the country from the mid-eighteenth century may have led women to develop a more prominent role than in the past, as I hope to show; but women had always had an economic role within Muslim society, although we still do not know how large that role was with any certainty since research into women's property is still in its toddler, if not infant, stage.

Because of the weakness of the administration, resulting from so many contenders for power among the elite households from the mid-eighteenth century to the end of the century, resources could not be fully controlled by the elites, who were otherwise occupied in warring against each other or against an outside force such as French, English, and Ottoman forces. As a consequence women, ulama, merchants, and the upper strata of the peasantry benefited by exploiting available resources.

If we assume that in a decentralized society many were able to control resources, then the opposite must have held: when the administration effectively centralized the resources of the country then only those groups targeted by it benefited—the rest, mostly women and ulama, became marginalized, as we shall see.

2

POLITICAL STRUGGLES
The Search for Leadership

During the eighteenth century society was divided into (1) the alien ruling elites—the mamluks (an Arabic term meaning "owned," a military oligarchy of imported slaves who were then manumitted) and the Ottoman suzerains of Egypt; and (2) native-born elites of ulama and *tujjar* (long-distance merchants who dealt in international luxury goods). Some North African, Ottoman, and Yemeni ulama and merchants were counted among the Egyptian elites by the population. Only the affluent merchants and the high ulama were elites.

The rest merged to form the next group of society: (3) the artisans and the rural affluent peasants (*fallahin*) and village heads (*shaikhs al-balad* or *umdas*), some of whom were richer than others; and (4) the poorer segments of urban and rural society.

The same stratification also applied to members of the religious minorities. Although there were no Christian or Jewish mamluks (since they were converted to Islam as soon as they were bought), there were rich and poor among the minorities, Christian and Jewish artisans, and poor Christian peasants.

As background it makes good sense to examine the power structure and control of economic resources in Egypt. From the mid-thirteenth century the mamluks, a kind of Praetorian guard, seized power and ruled the country until the Ottoman occupation in 922/1516. Mamluks perpetuated a system of government whereby children were bought as slaves and trained in households owned by manumitted mamluks, much as medieval barons trained squires, manumitted them as teenagers, and formed them into a cadre of administrators and warriors. The system did not allow freeborn natives to become mamluks. With some exceptions, freeborn sons of manumitted mamluks were not technically regarded as

17

mamluks and did not enter the military ranks in the eighteenth century, but merged with the population, becoming known as "sons of someone" (*awlad al-nas*).

Freeborn Egyptians became second-class citizens in a society which prized slave origins and their military valor. The mamluks' reason for being was to defend Egypt from foreign invasions, which they did successfully, repelling Mongols and Crusaders, until they were defeated by the Ottomans. The mamluks, a brilliant cavalry, refused to use firearms offensively since that contravened their code and were devastated by the Ottomans' use of the modern technology of the day: cannons and firearms.

The Ottomans did not destroy the mamluk system but incorporated it into their own system of government, which included a class of slaves who formed the military and much of the bureaucracy of the Ottoman Empire. The mamluks, all trained military men, were given auxiliary functions to help the Ottoman ruling elite in Egypt, such as collecting taxes in rural areas.

Ottoman Egypt was ruled by a governor—the *wali* or pasha—sent from Istanbul on yearly tenure. The governor had no control over the six Ottoman regiments, the *ocaqs*, who only obeyed their regimental commanders. Among them the janissaries and the Azabs were the elite infantry regiments. Most of the governors were content to act as arbiters in interregimental quarrels or intermamluk fights. Others had sufficient charisma or strength of character to play an effective administrative role.

The head of the regiments was called the *aga*. The *ocaqs* were divided into companies each headed by an officer, who rose from one rank in a regiment to a higher rank, sometimes in another regiment.

During the last decades of the seventeenth century janissaries who had intermarried with local women from among the artisanal groups enrolled their sons into the regiments, which thus became somewhat Egyptianized. Janissaries, the richest regiment, gained much of their wealth from a 5–7 percent impost on estates of deceased artisans and merchants. While exploiting the artisans, the regiments also protected them from too many extortions and too much taxation.[1] The head of the janissaries was the chief of the police (*mustahfazan*) in Cairo, as well as head of the army. A good number of the women discussed here were married to men from the *mustahfazan*.

The leading mamluk grandees were known as beys or amirs, the modern equivalent of a brigadier general,[2] or *sancaq*, a military position entitling the holder to plant a pole flying two horsetails outside his residence and to have a three-piece orchestra playing, as an outward sign of his rank.

Below the grandees, or two-horsetail *sancaqs*, some sixty to seventy mamluks held the title of *kashif* The exact function of the *kashifs* is not quite clear. Generally they occupied administrative positions in the provinces; but since there were only thirty-six such positions, the *kashifs* alternated them. The revenues of the *kashifs* came to one-third or one-half those of the grandees.[3] *Kashifs* formed the support system of the beys since they were members of beylical households promoted to that rank.

The eighteenth century began with a plague and a mammoth insurrection, known as the Grand Rebellion, in 1711. This uprising pitted the regiments against one another because of quarrels over the distribution of tax-farms, the sources of wealth and power, resulting in the eventual decimation of their leadership. The power vacuum thus created was filled by the mamluks, who entered the regiments and divided into factions which contested leadership. The beys, numbering some two dozen, became the real leaders of the country, with the Ottoman governor little more than a puppet, summarily dismissed when he displeased the mamluks.

Each mamluk grandee headed a household comprising an executive officer, his second-in-command (the *katkhoda* or *kikhya* as the Egyptians called him), a treasurer (the *khazindar*), various other minor officials, and a large number of young mamluks, bought and trained by the bey and his older officers in the art of warfare. Because mamluks were trained military men, they were able to displace the authority structure in the regiments. From the mid-eighteenth century the differences between regiments and mamluks no longer existed: they all followed the mamluk system.

Members of the same mamluk household treated each other as brothers and regarded their master (*ustadh*) as their father.[4] The mamluk household served the same function as kin-corporate groups before state formation. As with many blood relations, that closeness did not imply absolute loyalty: frequently the mamluk brothers fought one another and fought their master when the temptation to seize power became too strong. Members of the same mamluk household generally sided together against other households and formed the support groups of the leading beys. The beys tied their men to themselves by disbursing largesse in the way of tax-farms (*iltizams*) or salaries to their supporters. Each Ottoman regiment had been apportioned certain tax-farms to be disbursed in salaries to its members. Conflicts arose over the apportionment of tax-farms, especially new ones, since wealth was the road to power and hence to supremacy among the various mamluk households.

The ethnicity of the mamluks was diverse, reflecting the multiracial configuration of the Ottoman Empire: Armenians, Bosnians, Circassians, Georgians, Greeks, Laz, and Russians as well as Sudanese and some West Europeans. The same diverse ethnicity characterized mamluk women.

Such diverse ethnicity provided little common ground. Mamluks often did not even possess a common language until they learned Turkish to enable them to communicate with one another and some Arabic to enable them to carry out their religious duties, for they were converted to Islam as soon as they entered a household.

It is likely that most mamluk women also did not speak Arabic when they first arrived in the country, though they may have learned it later. We know, for example, that many harem women of the nineteenth century could barely speak any Arabic at all. Whatever their ethnicity, male and female mamluks communicated in Turkish, which had become the language of the military from the time of the early Abbassis.

By 1161/1748 two mamluks of the Qazdaghli faction established themselves as a duumvirate ruling over the country: Ibrahim Katkhoda, who headed the janissaries, and Ridwan Katkhoda, who headed the Azabs. For a brief while they held power and gave the country stability; when they died in 1168/1754 their followers, competing for power among themselves, ushered in a period of distress and instability from 1754 to 1174/1760. No one mamluk was strong enough to dominate the rest, until the advent of Ali Bey, surnamed the Great (al-Kabir). Both before and after his reign, the mamluk households were constantly in a state of unrest, fighting each other for power, wealth, and supremacy, which often escaped them.

The system of raising children to become mamluks changed during the reign of Ali Bey. Many of the mamluks who came to Egypt during the last four decades of the century did not learn Arabic, whereas in the past they had learned to speak it and could thus communicate freely with the local elites. Ali Bey brought in fully mature mercenaries as mamluks. In his hurry to develop an instant army to embark on his acquisition of an empire through conquest, he could not wait for youths to grow up and mature in the mamluk system.

The strongest bond holding the mamluks together as a group was self-interest; this is the case for most people, yet that bond is generally supplemented and sustained by family and regional or village relationships, which the mamluks lacked. The major characteristic of mamluks was their rootlessness: they had no family support system, but invented one for themselves—the mamluk household, which performed the same functions. The acquisition of power—and material wealth which bolstered power—and a system which allowed them a free hand in ruling the country were the only constants for the males. The females sought the accumulation of wealth as a hedge against the death of a protector (patron or husband).

The main land revenues came from customs dues and urban and rural tax-farms. By the end of the eighteenth century the military controlled over 60 percent of the customs dues and four-fifths of the rural tax-farms and invested in commercial constructions such as *wikalas*, baths, and shops. Out of 412 million *paras* of land taxes, the imperial treasury received a mere 88 million.[5] Some mamluks such as Muhammad Bey Charkas were reported to have had an annual revenue of 25 million *paras*.[6] While riches during the earlier part of the century came from tax-farms (*iltizams*), during the latter part they were derived more from urban sources, which were easier to exploit.

All agricultural land was, in theory, crown domain. This was divided into various lots and turned into tax-farms, which were originally instituted as a means of paying the military and collecting taxes without the expense of hiring tax collectors. Periodically, every three or so years, tax-farms were put up for auction to the highest bidder, who paid a fee in advance, roughly equivalent to the estimated taxes for one year to be collected from the peasants. The potential tax-farmer therefore had to possess enough ready cash to pay the auction fee, even when it was paid in installments. These individual plots were divided into twenty-four subdivisions (*qirats*), which had no definite size, varying from plot to plot. The land forming the tax-farm was of two different areas. The greater portion was land farmed by the villagers, who then paid the tax-farmer the tax specified by the Ottoman government, the *miri*. The tax-farmer kept a portion of the land tax as a fee for collecting the taxes, remitting the remainder to the treasury. The lesser part of the tax-farm was a piece of land known as *usya* (pl. *awasi*), incorrectly transliterated as *wasiya* by H. A. R. Gibb and Harold Bowen (vol. 1, p. iin183), which has confused non-Arabic speakers. They define it as seigniorial land, including the peasants as part of a corvée imposed on them, whose revenue went to the tax-farmer free of taxation.

Though tax-farms legally did not constitute private property by the middle of the eighteenth century, they were treated as such and were bought, sold, and mortgaged.[7] Auctioning the land posed a problem because ready cash was not as available to the mamluks as in the past. By then they had increased in numbers and were fighting each other over tax-farms and wealth. The grandees spent much money importing luxury goods and weapons and had little to spare. Anyone, military or civilian, with ready cash was encouraged to bid for a tax-farm. In 1732 women become registered as tax-farmers for the first time, along with ulama and merchants.[8]

Throughout the second half of the century the mamluk tax-farmers often added illegal taxes when they needed more funds. These taxes were registered and named the "extraordinary tax" or the "supplementary tax," to distinguish them from the only truly legal tax imposed by the Ottoman government, the *miri*. By this time the illegal taxes far outpaced the legal ones, and many of the legal taxes never even reached the imperial treasury (see Chapter 5). Such supplementary taxation was possibly necessary because the administration had relinquished tax collection to the tax-farmers, who kept the greater share; the administration had no option but to raise extra taxes or to send a punitive expedition, which happened only once. In addition, the income of the tax-farmers was declining and they were forced to shift their markets from internal to export and to raise further levies on the peasants and the urban artisans.

While the central government in Istanbul was imposing extra taxes in its other provinces because of imperial needs, in Egypt the rise in land taxes was inspired by the needs of the mamluks. Paying little attention to the central government, the mamluks on occasion deferred remitting taxes to the imperial treasury, pleading lack of funds. The need to raise more taxes was a consequence of the lack of a strong hand at the helm of government in Egypt. Weak grandees unsuccessfully vied for supreme power. All grandees needed more money to bribe their men to remain loyal, to woo others into joining their forces, or to buy weapons to arm themselves against opposing factions. In these turbulent times government was not only decentralized, but often ephemeral: a number of contenders competed for leadership, none becoming strong enough to dominate the rest. The Ottoman establishment could do little since the governor had no power of sanction and no popular support.

Meanwhile the economic system of land tenure and tax-farming was decreasing the funds available to the mamluks; some could no longer pay the taxes owed and lost their farms. One of the consequences of such a system as the tax-farm, where the peasant lived on a subsistence economy but owed the landlord certain working dues, was that profits were bound to vary, dropping when prices rose. The peasant could pay off the dues by producing less; therefore fewer commodities were marketed.[9] The tax-farmers tried various strategies to increase their share of production, such as producing a single commercial crop (rice or sugarcane) and, later, shifting their markets from domestic to foreign. The third strategy was to wrest land from others, which was the cause of the constant mamluk feuds that were characteristic of that age. Tax-farms shrank in size, with a tendency toward joint ownership. Whereas in the seventeenth century the number of *iltizams* in the provinces came to a total of 1,714, a century later the number had risen to 4,420, 250 percent of the previous total.[10]

Urban money-producing institutions were also tax farmed: the customs, both riverain and marine, and certain markets. In the late eighteenth century the urban taxes from Cairo alone were higher than the land taxes for the entire province of Egypt.[11] Such an increase could only mean a greater degree of exploitation of the urban sectors.

Since the elite controlled much of the wealth, they also maintained a certain form of noblesse oblige. They fed the poor and clothed the needy on religious occasions and invariably endowed some part of their property, with the income to be expended on charitable works. To show off their wealth and generosity toward the masses and their accessibility to the public, every grandee's household boasted two kitchens, one for the men and one for the women. Twice a day tables were set up and anyone who wished could enter the house and partake of a meal alongside the grandee and his male household. After the meal was over, when all the others had left, anyone could present a request to the grandee. The public thus had access to the highest in the land.

The same open-house system existed for women, operated by wives and relatives of grandees and attended by females only. It was customary for women to plead with more powerful women for favors for their husbands and for females to act as intermediaries between the men of their families and the grandees. (The custom exists to the present day and can be traced back to the early days of Islam.)

According to Jabarti, the mamluks held the ulama, the accepted native leaders of the population, in high esteem and respected the mores of the country. This resulted in a certain amount of give and take (*akhdh wa atta*) between the elites and the rest of the population.[12] Yet when the "take" exceeded the acceptable limits, when exploitation became too extreme, the population rose in revolt. The ulama then interceded to settle the conflict and in some sense to negotiate a redistribution of wealth. Matters proceeded peaceably enough until the next incident was triggered by some new action. Toward the end of the century new kinds of mamluks were brought into the country who had little respect for traditional ways and who created a need for a greater exploitation of financial resources.

Throughout the eighteenth century revolts broke out every ten or fifteen years,[13] apparently motivated by excessive or rising levels of exploitation on the part of the mamluks and an attempt to mitigate them on the part of the abused population. By the middle of the century the revolts arose not only because of increased exploitation but also because political and economic circumstances were changing. New groups were trying to make a place for themselves and wanted a share of the pie. Egyptian trade was beginning to turn toward Europe, although European trade was only 15 percent of the total, the bulk of trade being with the Ottoman Empire. A cash crop economy was also developing. Rice was grown in Damietta in a protocapitalist manner, where merchants financed peasants to grow the crop for export. In middle Egypt tax-farmers were developing sugarcane and indigo production.

The major change in trade, commerce, and political direction came in the latter half of the eighteenth century, the catalyst being Ali Bey al-Kabir. In 1760 Ali Bey, a former mamluk of Ibrahim Katkhoda, the duumvir who had ruled in 1748, came to power as *shaikh al-balad*. This was a title given to the premier bey and had nothing to do with the same title given to a village elder. Once he was established as *primus inter pares*, Ali Bey attempted to rise above that level and to centralize all power in his hands. In order to establish himself as the sole authority in the country he exiled his former supporters and opponents or exterminated them unless they accepted him as sole ruler. These actions galvanized resistance toward him on the part of the grandees, who managed to defeat and banish him in 1766.

While in exile Ali Bey roused support for himself and regained power the following year. From then on he became an absolute ruler determined to centralize resources, quell latent opposition, and plan expansion beyond his frontiers and along the major trade routes. His actions not only became a blueprint followed later by Muhammad Ali, but increased the paucity of true leadership among the mamluks, causing constant internecine quarrels among the beylicate during the next decades. This constant warfare among beys resulted in a growing need for ready cash to retain supporters by giving them more funds and to buy weaponry from Europe. To pay the retainers and buy weapons the mamluks sold their tax-farms, so that more and more women, ulama, and *tujjar* figured among the list of tax-farmers.

Factional strife had begun long before Ali Bey but accelerated after his reign. Also, because of such political turmoil the grandees could not pay as much attention to economic matters as they had in the past and left this to their women. Women therefore were allowed to participate in the marketplace more freely than in the past, selling crops, investing in trade and commerce, buying shops, and so forth. One might also conjecture that mamluk wives were encouraged by their menfolk to accumulate wealth in their own names since males could be disinherited by their opponents when they fell from power, but women were usually left untouched (although there were many exceptions to such treatment, as we shall see).

When the French under Bonaparte landed in Egypt in 1798, they asked Husain Effendi, the administrator of the registration tax, a series of questions regarding administrative matters in Egypt. When asked who the main tax-farmers in Egypt were, he reported that "in recent times, most of the tax-farms went to the women," whereas the previous owners had been the military, the mamluks, religious men, merchants, and women.[14] Husain Effendi was exaggerating when he said the main tax-farmers were women, but he was right in believing that many women held tax-farms, although they had not held them before 1145/1732.

The second long period of factional strife was in 1775–1798, when many mamluks bought tax-farms in the names of their wives or their manumitted slaves or sold them cheaply to women.[15]

Where in the registers of tax-farmers in 1069–1071/1658–1660 the majority were military men (1,561 or 91.1 percent), the remainder being "Arabs and others," meaning tribal shaikhs plus a few ulama, a century later the picture changes. Out of a total of 4,420 tax-farmers in 1212/1797, the military numbered 2,616 or 59.2 percent, a decrease of 31.9 percent (bearing in mind that the tax-farms were smaller in size); tribal shaikhs numbered 860 or 19.5 percent; women numbered 580 or 13.1 percent; ulama numbered 307 or 6.9 percent; while merchants numbered 57 or 1.3 percent.[16]

The major economic change other than in land tenure came around 1760. Syrian Melkite merchants, escaping from persecution of their sect by the non-Catholic Christian elements in their homeland, from 1730 sought refuge in Egypt, a country with which they had previously traded.[17] Seeking to make a place for themselves in trade, these merchants displaced many of the European, especially French, merchants. They eventually managed to monopolize trade in cloth. In time they also displaced old *tujjar*—Egyptian, Moroccan, and Jewish—and introduced new ways of doing business. Ali Bey, who distrusted the old customs officials, mostly Jewish, because of their close links with the janissaries, was amenable to the suggestions of the new Syrian émigrés regarding new methods of taxing the customs. The Syrians displaced the Jews and extorted more funds from the customs, which the bey needed to finance his expeditions abroad. The Syrian merchants took advantage of the need for raw materials at the beginning of the Industrial Revolution in Europe, especially in England and France. They convinced Ali Bey and his successors that it made more sense, and cash, to export raw materials rather than to export the finished textiles, which had been a major Egyptian money maker. Thus Syrians and grandees together manipulated the market, raising the price of raw cotton and diminishing the price of textiles, which undermined the production of textiles, the foremost industry in the country. Furthermore, they sought to redirect trade toward Europe instead of toward the Ottoman Empire, for they could get more funds from that source. Europe needed foodstuffs, such as rice and sugarcane and also dyes and indigo, all of which were slowly becoming major money-making crops in Egypt.

Ali Bey's military expeditions were to earn him the animosity of the Ottomans, especially when he conquered the Hijaz, the major trade route for Egypt, but also the region of the Muslim Holy Cities and the goal of the richest caravan, the pilgrimage caravan of the Ottomans. When his next step was to conquer Syria, the Ottomans sent an army against him, bribed his righthand man to betray him, and brought about his demise.

Ali Bey was not the only local ruler to seek autonomy from the Ottomans. Others did the same thing, a phenomenon that Albert Hourani has identified as the "politics of the Notables."[18] Governors of provinces, enticed by the growing need for raw materials, sought to expand their commercial linkages with Europe. The fastest way to do that was to impose a control on agricultural resources that verged on the monopolistic and to redirect agriculture toward cash crops for export. In many cases these efforts resulted in a revitalization of territories by local rulers setting themselves up as quasi-independent governors. Dhahir al-Umar in Galilee and Jezzar Ahmad in Acre were examples. The Porte, enmeshed in financial and military problems, was in no condition to retaliate against such "upstarts" so long as they remained within the imperial fold and remitted tribute.

Ali Bey had broken that unwritten law; hence the Ottomans took steps to put him down. Ali Bey was betrayed by his favorite and former treasurer, Muhammad Bey Abu-l Dhahab, whom the Ottomans appointed as the new chief bey in 1772. Muhammad had been promoted to *sanjaq* in 1177/ 1763 by Ali Bey. On that occasion, instead of distributing silver coins among the populace as was customary, he distributed gold coins, which earned him his sobriquet Abu-l Dhahab, "the father of gold."

For the brief period during which Muhammad Bey reigned, the country prospered. Jabarti noted that matters were not bad—they were even satisfactory[19]—but the bey died suddenly in 1189/1775.

From then until the end of the century Egypt was to be rent by constant unrest. According to Jabarti, Muhammad Bey's mamluks were an unruly and undisciplined lot and their behavior brought evil and calamities to the land. There was constant fighting among the grandees, two of whom, Murad Bey and Ibrahim Bey, eventually managed to dominate the rest. Neither grandee was strong enough to exterminate or outmaneuver the other; they ruled most of the time as a second duumvirate, but frequently were at loggerheads, attempting to oust one another. Some historians in the past believed that such fighting was motivated by a senseless blood lust, but it makes more sense to see it as motivated by a need to grab a larger share of the financial pie in order to pay off retainers and buy weapons and above all to make up for the shortfall of revenue derived from land.

Where in the past the mamluks had resided in the villages and supervised their lands, they were now city based, in order to be close to the center of power and thus protect their interests. They used agents to collect their rents, usually *umdas* and village shaikhs, who kept some of these rents for themselves. Thus an inner dynamic within the country was creating new conditions for money making and for expanding power at the expense of the old power structure. Prices of wheat and rice were rising to their highest levels from 1778 onward, which also meant that peasants could pay off their corvée labor on land faster than usual; consequently production of cereals for the market fell.

The Ottomans attempted to reconquer Egypt from the duumvirs, who had neglected to remit the tribute for the past years, and in 1786 sent a punitive expedition against the beys headed by Qapudan Jazairli Hasan Pasha, the admiral of the fleet. Hasan Pasha unsuccessfully sought to end the duumvirate and only succeeded in chasing the duumvirs into upper Egypt. It was a mamluk stratagem when they feared losing a battle to retreat south to upper Egypt, Nubia, and the Sudan. Once the opposing army had withdrawn to Cairo—for few invading armies (including the French) had the manpower to hold onto all of Egypt or to leave behind effective garrisons which could repel the mamluks—the beys returned to control upper Egypt, the major grain-producing area, thereby dominating the food resources of the capital. The duumvirs returned to power the year after the Ottoman army evacuated Egypt, for the empire was about to begin another round in the endless Ottoman-Russian wars and needed Hasan Pasha and his men.

Not only was the government, whether in mamluk or Ottoman hands, chaotic and exploitative of the population, but a number of natural disasters also swept the country, wreaking even more havoc than had the mamluks. In 1198–1199/1783–1784 the Nile flood was low, resulting in drought. Worse still, Murad and Ibrahim were fighting, each stationed on one bank of the Nile, so navigation was impossible and little food could reach the capital. Famine broke out in the summer and continued into the following year. It was rumored that 500 people a day died from the famine.[20] This was followed by a plague which broke out in 1785; the number of victims was said to reach 1,500 a day.[21]

In 1791 plague once more appeared, this time killing between 1,500 and 2,000 a day. Fourteen *sancaq* beys were killed,[22] but this allowed the remainder to redistribute the wealth.[23] In 1792 an atrocious famine broke out; Jabarti claimed that people resorted to eating corpses of animals in the street and even to cannibalism.[24] It was estimated that over the last two decades of the century over one-third of the population had died through plague or famine. The following years witnessed repeated popular uprisings. The coin of the day, the *nisf fidda* or *para*, was devalued by 50 percent from 1750 to 1791. Its value was stable from 1786 to 1791, then fell again; in terms of constant paras, 100 paras in 1678 were only worth 32 *paras* a century later.[25] When Bonaparte's savants studied Egypt, later producing the monumental work *Description de l'Egypte*, they found a country that was depopulated, economically depressed, and in political disarray. The French occupation did not help matters, since it was a further exploitation of resources; it resulted in an Anglo-Ottoman expedition to Egypt to oust the French in 1801, at the cost of further devastating the land.

(See Table 1 on following page)

Table 1. Evolution of the *Para* from 1670 to 1798
(Indices for 1681–1688 = 100)

1670	117	1705	93	1740	63	1775	55
1	115	6	89	1	61	6	55
2	108	7	—	2	63	7	—
3	110	8	91	3	—	8	55
4	112	9	80	4	64	9	55
1675	105	1710	—	1745	64	1780	—
6	100	1	—	6	62	1	55
7	105	2	79	7	62	2	55
8	105	3	69	8	—	3	—
9	105	4	67	9	61	4	—
1680	105	1715	66	1750	61	1785	—
1	100	6	77	1	61	6	48
2	100	7	80	2	62	7	—
3	100	8	83	3	61	8	47
4	100	9	85	4	61	9	46
1685	100	1720	64	1755	61	1790	—
6	100	1	62	6	62	1	47
7	100	2	58	7	—	2	46
8	100	3	51	8	—	3	45
9	98	4	58	9	61	4	—
1690	95	1725	49	1760	60	1795	36
1	92	6	47	1	60	6	30
2	90	7	—	2	61	7	30
3	89	8	—	3	60	8	32
4	85	9	—	4	60		
1695	88	1730	56	1765	—		
6	85	1	—	6	60		
7	83	2	—	7	60		
8	83	3	68	8	60		
9	83	4	69	9	—		
1700	77	1735	—	1770	60		
1	77	6	67	1	59		
2	77	7	67	2	58		
3	47	8	—	3	58		
4	93	9	66	4	55		

Source: André Raymond, *Artisans et commerçants au Caire au XVIIIème siècle,* vol. 1, p. 42.

Among the military in the Anglo-Ottoman expedition was a young officer, Muhammad Ali, who with the connivance of the ulama succeeded in ridding the country of the mamluks and the Ottoman forces and in setting up a centralized government that was eventually to create an Egyptian state.

The general economic picture of Egypt in the sixteenth to eighteenth centuries varied between times when surplus was monopolized by the redistributive system and a period of transition when surplus tended toward marketlike transactive exchanges. Victor Nee (in "A Theory of Market Transition," which examines the situation in communist China as it changed from one system of allocation to another) hypothesizes that two things are likely to happen when surplus is no longer monopolized by the redistributive system and more is allocated and distributed through marketlike exchanges. First, the central system has less control over resources and therefore can exert less power. Direct producers acquire more power over the terms of exchange; consequently there is a transfer of power which favors the direct producers in relation to the redistributors. Second, markets provide incentive and new opportunities, giving rise to entrepreneurial groups as an alternative to bureaucratic advancement in the state system.[26]

I believe that this hypothesis is applicable to Egypt in the eighteenth and nineteenth centuries. The sixteenth century, when the Ottoman authorities maintained power in Egypt, was a redistributive phase when the administration set the prices for transactions, monopolized the output by administrative fiat, then redistributed the goods to the public. Advancement for those not in the alien elites (the Ottoman/mamluk hierarchy) was either through the military or through the bureaucracy.

During the second phase, the transitional second half of the eighteenth century, the power of the administration was diminished and divided among a number of contenders, causing the redistributive abilities to

---

Note: The table on the facing page contains information from the registers of the *Mahkama.* The index of the *para* was obtained by combining the indices of the *bundugi* and *riyal,* calculated according to their value during the years 1681 to 1688 as the period of reference (base 100): 105 *paras* for the *bundugi* and 50 *paras* for the *riyal.* For these two coins their maximal values registered in the sources were taken into account.

For the *riyal,* no distinction was made between the rate of exchange of the Spanish piastre and the *Thaler.*

weaken and prices to become set by the market exchanges and not by administrative fiat. Hence the administration lost some of its powers of coercion and manipulation of the market, allowing direct producers to acquire more power and new groups to rise as entrepreneurs. This explains the increase in numbers of merchants, women, and ulama as landholders in the eighteenth century. It also accounts for the opportunities for women to accumulate wealth and invest in the market.

Once the redistributive power was again monopolized by the state, as under Muhammad Ali (1220–1264/1805–1848), then the new entrepreneurs disappeared from the scene; once again prices were set by the administration, and advancement in the bureaucracy became the only alternative. One consequence of a more centralized state administration which determined who was to gain benefits from the new systems instituted was the marginalization of certain groups in society, such as women and the peasantry. The women who had participated in the marketplace were displaced by the state, and the peasants became wage laborers; land became de facto private property, distributed at the whim of the head of the state, to be granted to his supporters and bureaucrats. The mamluks also sustained losses. Their options were to join the new state as bureaucrats, leave the country, or be killed in battle. The new regime established in the nineteenth century was a centralized state under the strong direction of one who can be called "the last of the mamluks" as well as the first of the modern centralized rulers.

3

SOCIETY IN MAMLUK EGYPT
The Elites

Marriage in Islam is not a sacrament but a civil contract between a male and a female—though the female is frequently represented by her father or her uncle. When females were married at a very young age, at the onset of puberty, and had little knowledge of finances or dowries, men assumed that they needed an older male to look after their interests. Thus the contract was negotiated between the guardian of the bride and the groom, or his guardian if he was under age. Some schools of jurisprudence insisted that a woman was incapable of acting on her own and must be represented and given in marriage by a guardian; other schools, such as the Maliki, believed that if a woman was an adult she could conduct her own negotiations herself and was entitled to give herself in marriage to whomever she pleased.

Because marriage is a civil transaction, not a religious one, some schools of jurisprudence allow terms to be specified in the contract dealing with the amount of dowry to be paid by the male. In theory that dowry represented the bride's capital, her own property, to be supplemented by whatever funds her parents gave her. The contract also included a back dowry to be paid to the bride in case of divorce; generally the back dowry specified a large amount as punitive damages in case of repudiation. If the woman herself demanded a divorce, then she forfeited the back dowry. Contracts from the eighteenth century mentioned many other details indicating prior negotiations between the two parties.[1] For example, in one contract the bride specified that she be permitted to visit her mother whenever she wished and that she had the right to wear whatever she pleased. Then as now there were even contracts which spelled out the woman's right to divorce her husband should he take another wife.[2]

The financial nature of marriage as a transaction was made clearer when the marriage was enjoined to be between social equals, for the husband had to support the wife in the manner to which she was accustomed. Should he have more than one wife, he must treat his bride equally with his other wives and supply her with the same comforts. Unequal treatment was grounds for divorce. Marriage entitled the wife to be totally supported by her husband. Whatever property she possessed when she entered the marriage, or acquired after, was hers to do with as she pleased; her spouse, theoretically, was not entitled to touch any part of it without her permission.

Unmarried females, a rare occurrence in the past, were to be supported by male family members. If they had no such relatives, then the state was supposed to support them, but usually did not. Many charitable endowments were set up to support females who were destitute and to supply them with trousseaus upon marriage.

Financial arrangements were thus an important part of the marriage contract and one of the few elements of leverage that a female possessed. While a woman could be verbally repudiated by her husband, who pronounced a threefold "I divorce thee" formula, she had to sue for divorce in a court of law and show cause. Once the woman was divorced, her former husband had to pay the back dowry specified in the marriage contract unless the woman had renounced her claim to it. The husband was also expected to give back all the property the spouse had brought to the marriage: her household chattels, gifts, and jewelry. The husband had to pay child support until the children reached the age of puberty or whatever age the different schools of law specified, when they went into the father's custody.

Jack Goody believes that societies in which women received property through inheritance or through a dowry developed a strong tendency to control marriages. As he points out, an heiress cannot marry just anyone; her partner is more likely to have been chosen for her.[3] Such societies also placed a premium on premarital virginity and revealed a tendency toward homogamy,[4] both of which were enjoined in Islamic law, where extramarital sex was a major sin.

If a marriage between free individuals and social equals reflected an unequal power relationship, this was even more true of a marriage between apparent nonequals, as in the case of elite mamluk marriages. Frequently the mamluk wife had been bought by her husband or bought by another man and given as a present to the man who manumitted then married her. Or she might have remained the slave of one man, whose children she bore, then was given as a gift to another man. The habits of submission learned as a slave may not have changed easily to attitudes of authority in a marriage relationship once the woman was manumitted, at least vis-à-vis her husband during the first marriage. Power struggles within a marriage do not necessarily mean that the female was not able to manipulate the relationship. By the time the woman embarked on the second or third marriage she had acquired authority, at least in matters of economy. Or perhaps those women who showed powers of authority had never learned submission in the harem. Submission within a gender relationship did not necessarily imply submission in other relationships: mamluk women were certainly not submissive when it came to handling economic relationships, as we shall see.

Mamluk men had once been slaves when children, but had acquired habits of command with age and with military training. Perhaps women simulated overt submission as a public face presented to the master and covertly nurtured other qualities or channeled their authoritarian traits into the acquisition of wealth.

Such an anomalous situation of slaves becoming masters and of men constantly involved in warfare and thus away from their homes and their financial interests may have developed an implicit social contract between the spouses. The male amassed property by virtue of his position of power, and the female was entrusted with the growth and supervision of that property. The male led a public life, the female a private one; yet each had an impact on the other: the male brought some part of his public life into the harem, and the female influenced public life through her advice or requests in the privacy of the bedroom.

While this lies in the realm of speculation, such an implicit contract is suggested by the way in which mamluk wives managed their husbands' finances in their absence. They had access to their husbands' treasure, usually hidden in a secret chamber in the house, and could thus send funds whenever needed when their spouses were away. But if finances were managed by the women in the absence of the males, were finances managed by the women when the men were busy with public life?

It would be easy to jump to the conclusion that women became involved in making money as extraordinary means during critical times when chaos and political insecurity were rife, but that was not strictly true. Women took over the management of property not only in times of crisis and not only as a response to unusual circumstances. Many women controlled wealth before the eighteenth century. Carl Petry has shown that the wife of Qait Bey (873–902/1468–1496) had been trained by her father to become supervisor (na*zira*) of his *waqf,* over the head of her brother.[5] Thus the training of women to run financial interests (*awqaf* and other investments) was an old, established custom among the mamluk elite. The many trust deeds by women setting up endowments of various kinds or setting up commercial buildings and citing other investments indicate that women had always been involved in the financial and commercial life of the country. M. M. Amin found that 283 out of 1,000 deeds dating from 239/853 to 922/1516 were endowments made by women who supervised property inherited from husbands and fathers.[6] Later periods show an increase in such endowments on the part of women. It may be that in times of decentralized power women acquired a greater share of the economic pie than they would normally have had (in terms of degree of involvement, rather than involvement per se). When the Ottomans occupied Egypt in 922/1516 and during early times when there was a certain degree of stability in government and the Ottomans controlled the country's resources, women played a less prominent economic role, especially in regard to the ownership of tax-farms, which were strictly controlled by the military. We have no concrete evidence yet as to the extent of women's involvement in other commercial investments, but certainly women inherited, deeded, and endowed property.

Throughout the Muslim world, as noted above, women inherited property, for that right was specified in the Quran. There is, however, a difference between legally owning property and actively managing the property and controlling the income derived from it. Because women of the property-owning sectors were cloistered, it was assumed that they had no role in the marketplace or that their role was limited to a handful of elite women, who always had a choice. We now find that women of all social groups were involved in the marketplace. In a society which was preindustrial and which had not developed a centralized state system, the economic role of women was broader and more dynamic and went far beyond the passive role of a consumer.

In an interesting article on Ottoman women, Ian C. Dengler points out the public role that women of the elite played: "[they] had one role not open to other women in the social order: they could become political and social arbiters...women of the ruling elites...became heads of vast clientage and patronage networks that at times gave them direct control over the entire Ottoman state apparatus."[7] He goes on to add, citing Lady Mary Wortley Montagu, that women of the elite "had come to possess most of the advantages that Ottoman society could confer on individuals of Either [*sic*] sex: wealth, power, and virtually unlimited control over self, property and leisure time...free to spend their husbands' money as they might wish." Lady Mary Wortley Montagu may not have been the best source, although she saw a comparison between sexual attitudes among the Ottomans and British society of her day and was particularly sensible of wealth, of which she had little or none; but she saw enough to envy the "freedom" of Ottoman women as compared to European women.

Much of that description fits women of the mamluk elite in Egypt. Though they could not rule through their sons as Ottoman valides did, they did advise and guide their spouses. They certainly became social arbiters. As manumitted slaves, they could not be said to have unlimited control of themselves, but neither did women of the Sérail in Istanbul, who were also slave women. Nonetheless, married mamluk women had unlimited control over wealth and property. In spite of the fact that society was ostensibly divided into a public sphere for men and a private one for women, elite women developed networks in much the same fashion as did their men and penetrated the public sphere with ease.

We know, for example, that Nafisa Khatun married off her female slaves into most of the mamluk households and that these women appealed to her whenever they were in trouble.

Much activity that was not of a private nature was conducted in the harem. The strict demarcation of business in the office and pleasure at home was never adhered to in that society. Indeed, by the eighteenth century, when the mamluk grandees seized power, the center of government moved out of the citadel, the residence of the Ottoman *wali*, and into the mamluk household.

As Nelly Hanna has shown in her seminal study of habitations in Cairo during the seventeenth and the eighteenth centuries, the functions of houses changed. Mamluk residences acquired rooms referred to as *diwans*, sometimes even an inner and an outer *diwan*. *Diwans* were places where public affairs were normally conducted in the ruler's residence. This departure showed that power had moved from the residence of the Ottoman *wali* to the house of the premier bey of the day, the *shaikh al-balad*, who conducted the administration from his own residence. Palaces acquired a prison (*sign*), further reinforcing the bey's administrative power. Frequently executions and assassinations took place in the houses of grandees, thus forcibly intruding public life into what had previously been private space.

These public activities initiated a new element in the construction of beylical residences: apartments were set aside for the private use of the women in the household to prevent their witnessing or being exposed to such acts of violence. This division of the house into a male section and a female section was previously unknown in mamluk houses. It is only during the eighteenth century that such terms as "the women's gate" (*bab al-harim*) and even "the women's kitchen" (*matbakh al-harim*) begin to appear, which were totally unknown in the seventeenth century. Hanna claims the main difference between grandee houses in the seventeenth and the eighteenth centuries was a change of attitude toward the usage of space rather than any architectural changes. She shows that in the early eighteenth century only 2.5 percent of the houses had such elements as a gate for women, for power had not yet entirely been transferred from the Ottoman governor to the grandees; by the middle of the century that number had risen to 40 percent, while by the end of the century the term appears in 84 percent of these houses along with terms such as "the women's kitchen" and "the women's garden."[8]

Hanna notes "une tendance dans les palais de la classe militaire à constituer des entités autonomes, se suffisant pour les besoins de la vie quotidienne." As they became autonomous, beylical residences began to acquire mills, wells, and workshops in order to withstand sieges. She adds that terms such as "the women's quarters" (*haramlik*) and "the men's quarters" (*salamlik*), which were common in the other Ottoman regions, appeared in Egyptian houses only in the nineteenth century.[9]

The change in the use of space did not necessarily mean that women were more restricted in movement than before. It was simply a means of keeping the seedy side of mamluk life away from the women and children. It also meant a greater distancing between the males and the females; women may have had more freedom to act than heretofore, for they could come and go as they pleased without supervision, using their own gates. The greater distance between the sexes, however, might lead to women having less access to the males and to power. That is precisely what happened in the nineteenth century.

The houses of grandees also differed from those of the rest of the population in construction materials, making lavish use of marble and painted wood, and in the size and number of the rooms. It is said that the duumvir Abd al-Rahman Katkhoda in 1752 built a house which occupied two and a half acres of land in Bulaq costing 1,600,000 paras. Since it was totally destroyed there is no way to verify that allegation. But Hanna found some palaces with thirty-five rooms, while some had as many as five storage rooms (*hasik*), stables, two kitchens, two hallways (*qaas*), five areas (*riwaqs*), and a sitting area (*maqaad*).[10] By the end of the eighteenth century grandee houses often had more than one bath; some had two, while one had five.

Such a change in the use of space implied that the beylical house had acquired a further function than merely being a living quarter. Indeed, mamluk houses then included a whole new group of individuals tied to the household and service of the bey—such as the stable boy (*sayis*), cook (*tabbakh*), supervisor (*mubashir*), and scribe (*katib*)[11]—who moved out of the public area of the *suq* into the area of the household.

Nineteenth-century Western authors who discovered the "exoticism" of the "Orient" pictured Egyptian women either as sex objects as did Gérard de Nerval or as "odalisques" à la Ingres, reclining in harems and passing the time in intrigue and eating rahat lukum (Turkish delight). As Clot Bey wrote, "On s'imagine généralement en Europe qu'un harem est une sorte de lieu de prostitution, où le libertinage d'un peuple énervé a placé le théâtre exclusif des jouissances sensuelles les plus nombreuses et de la plus abrutissante débauche. On se trompe; un ordre sévère, une rigoureuse décence, règnent dans le harem, et font que, à bien des égards, il ressemble à nos établissements monastiques."[12]

One might well wonder where Clot got his information regarding harems, since the only harem to which he could have had access had to be his own; in no way did a harem resemble a monastic order, but it certainly was a place where order reigned, where everyone was assigned a task, and where administrative skills were necessary to direct and guide the numerous servants, slaves, and retainers. Even more importantly, some harem women showed entrepreneurial talents to the extent that they amassed more property and wealth than many males roaming freely in the marketplace. We know from their deeds or endowments that they invested in houses for rent, in wikalas, in shops of various kinds, in tax-farms—indeed in every venture that was open to an investor.

The participation of women in the marketplace may also have been a consequence of the system of education then available. Education, or literacy, was religious in nature. Ulama were the teachers of the day and taught any Muslim who asked. Among the elites it was customary to bring in an alim to teach reading, writing, and religion to the young mamluks. Learned women were brought into the harem to teach young female mamluks, who suffered from the same handicaps as the men—lack of knowledge of Islam and of a common language with their new masters. Being literate or illiterate had no role in whether one was capable of investing and creating wealth, which required knowledge of the marketplace and of commercial ventures. Much as in medieval Europe, where barons were illiterate and depended on monks and accountants to document their financial activities, mamluks may have done the same. Women were allowed a role in the marketplace, which greatly expanded when the men were busy elsewhere.

Before embarking on details showing the kinds of property that elite women accumulated, an examination of the way in which the mamluk system imposed certain social practices might help us understand the process of the accumulation of wealth. Much of the wealth of the grandees came from tax-farms of various kinds assigned to them by virtue of their public functions, which devolved on the next grandee when the first one died.

It was only the grandee's personal wealth, often considerable, accumu-lated during his lifetime by legal or illegal means which was inherited by his family. Thus a grandee daughter or widow was sure to inherit sizable amounts of property. Keeping property within the family was one of the reasons why many Muslim Egyptian families chose the father's brother's son as a spouse for a daughter.

Mamluks regarded the household as their only family until they married, so grandees frequently gave their daughters or sisters in marriage to the nearest equivalent to a nephew—the grandee's lieutenant (*katkhoda*) or the treasurer (*khazindar*), the bey's righthand men. The second in command would inherit the leadership of the household after the bey, for the mamluk system rarely permitted the son of a mamluk to succeed his father as the head of the household.

As noted, Jack Goody believes that when a society transfers property to women through marriage or inheritance, "a premium is placed upon in-marriage than [*sic*] out-marriage, upon endogamy rather than exogamy."[13] Claude Lévi-Strauss adds that women become objects "with which men seek to initiate and solidify relationships with each other. . . . men use [women] to enhance their political and economic interests through adroit marital alliances."[14] This was exactly the case with mamluk marriages.

There were numerous examples of such marriages. Ismail Bey al-Kabir gave his daughter in marriage to his treasurer, Ibrahim Aga, while Abu-l Dhahab Bey gave Yusif Bey, one of his amirs, his daughter in marriage.[15] Muhammad Shalabi Bey married one of his three daughters to his treasurer. When Muhammad Shalabi died, Ibrahim Katkhoda, his patron or *ustadh*, gave Muhammad's widow to Ibrahim's own treasurer, Mahmud Aga. When Mahmud Aga died, Ibrahim found the woman another husband, yet another of his retainers, Husain Aga, whom he named *kashif* of Mansura.[16] Beys made sure that whatever wealth their retainers had accumulated during their lifetime remained among the members of the household, so as much care was given to the marriage of widows as to that of daughters and sisters. Ali Bey al-Kabir gave his treasurer, Ismail Bey (whom he invested as *sancaq*), Hanim, the daughter of Ali's master—Ibrahim Katkhoda.[17] When Ismail died, Hanim was married to Ahmad Aga, another of her father's men;[18] when he died, she married Muhammad Aga al-Barudi, her deceased husband's treasurer.[19] There seems to have been a love story behind that marriage. Ahmad Aga had given Muhammad Aga, his treasurer, his daughter in marriage. When Ahmad Aga died, Muhammad repudiated his wife and married her stepmother, Hanim, thus becoming her third husband. Then Muhammad Aga gave his repudiated wife in marriage to Hasan Kashif and gave another of his patron's daughters in marriage to his own treasurer, Ali Bey. A further example of marriages between key personnel within a household and the ¯ ᵃale family members is Ismail Bey Abu Madfaa, who had been his .aster's treasurer and married his master's daughter.[20]

The widow of a grandee, who inherited part of his wealth, also became a prize. Frequently she married either the grandee's lieutenant, who became the new grandee, or his treasurer; the ruling amir might marry her himself or give her in marriage to one of his own men. Ali Bey al-Kabir married four wives. His chief wife, Aisha Kadin, had been a slave of Ibrahim Katkhoda, Ali's master. After Ali Bey's death she married Muhammad Bey Abu-l Dhahab, his successor and usurper. Another of Ali Bey's wives, the famous Nafisa Khatun, was later married by Murad Bey. We know nothing more about the other two wives, al-Sitt Munawwar Khatun and al-Sitt Gulsun.[21] Murad Bey had also been married to Fatima, widow of the amir Salih Bey, who died in 1768. The duumvir Ibrahim Bey had been married to the sister of his master, Muhammad Bey Abu-l Dhahab, who then gave Ibrahim Bey one of his own favorites, Amnatullah Khatun, in marriage.[22]

The widow could always refuse to marry the proposed suitor. Ismail Bey, brother of Ali Bey al-Ghazzawi and lieutenant of Muhammad Bey Abu-l Dhahab, married Fatima Hanim, the daughter of Ridwan Katkhoda, a duumvir who ruled with Ibrahim Katkhoda in the middle of the century. She had been engaged to be married to Ali Aga, one of her father's mamluks; the marriage contract had actually been written up, so that legally she was considered his spouse though the marriage had not yet been consummated. When Ali Aga went to Iraq and sent for his wife, she was reluctant to join him and consequently petitioned to have the marriage dissolved according to the Maliki school of jurisprudence. When the marriage was dissolved, she married Ismail. Later Ismail wished to marry a certain Salun, one of Ridwan's former concubines. Salun had been Ismail's sister-in-law, married to his brother Ali. When Ali died, Ismail asked for her hand in marriage, but she refused to marry him. Ismail then went to his patron, Abu-l Dhahab, and recounted his tale of woe. Abu-l Dhahab explained that Salun might have refused to marry him out of a sense of propriety since he was already married to her former owner's daughter, Fatima Khatun, and she, a former concubine, would not set herself up next to her master's daughter. At Ismail's insistence Abu-l Dhahab interceded with the woman, who finally agreed to marry Ismail, perhaps because pressure was put on her or because Ismail's first wife was already ill and dying, which she did soon after, or because she wanted to marry the man and put up a front *pour la forme*.[23]

The later duumvir Ibrahim Bey married his daughter Adila to Ibrahim Bey the Younger, one of his men. The husband died during the battle of Imbaba (1213/1798) so in 1216/1801 Ibrahim Bey gave his daughter in marriage to Sulaiman Kashif, who had been her dead husband's mamluk.[24]

This brings us to the question of whether these women were consulted as to their marriages or were simply married off. As in most elite houses in Europe, marriage was an alliance, and the views of the bride were rarely taken into consideration, especially if she was a slave or the young daughter of the household. There is evidence that widows had a choice of whom to marry among their husband's retainers or allies. They may have chosen a treasurer or a lieutenant because they were better acquainted with them than with other maluks—and they were certainly the most powerful men within the household. If her former husband's master chose to give her in marriage to one of his retainers it would have been impolitic to refuse, unless, of course, she hastened to choose her own spouse herself or, better yet, nudged the grandee into proposing the man she wanted as a marriage partner.

One account by Jabarti in 1217/1802–1803 listed six mamluks who married the wives or daughters of their patrons.[25] Sulaiman Bey, a mamluk of Ibrahim Bey, married his master's daughter Adila. Abd al-Rahman Kashif, mamluk of Uthman Bey al-Muradi, married his master's widow. Umar Kashif, mamluk of Uthman Bey al-Ashqar, married his master's widow. Muhammad Kashif, a mamluk of Sulaiman Bey al-Aga, married his master's daughter. Ismail Kashif, a mamluk of Rashwan Bey, married his master's widow, Zainab, daughter of the amir Ibrahim Bey. Abd al-Rahman Kashif, who had belonged to Uthman Bey al-Tamburji, married his widow. Umar, Sulaiman, Ismail, and Abd al-Rahman all became *sancaq* beys.

Jabarti, who was generally uninterested in women's doings, went into detail regarding marriages of mamluks because in his period such marriages reinforced the close ties that existed between members of the same household, even when they had left that household and set up for themselves. Marriage cemented alliances, much as they did in elite systems elsewhere. They were generally an expression of power relationships more than a question of personal need or choice.

Often marriages were arranged within the same household or among members of the same household. To give one's concubine in marriage to a retainer was not considered an insult but rather a great compliment, for it tied the retainer closer to his patron, since the concubine remained close to the other women of the bey's household even after she had gone to another household. The relationship between a patron and his client/slave remained even when the former slave became manumitted and rose in rank and power. When Muhammad Bey, husband of the thrice-wed Hanim, became a widower, Murad Bey gave him in marriage one of his own concubines, his prime favorite and the mother of his son, Ayyub. Thus networks were built up within households and across households. In my research I found that only five of the women in the list of elite women were bought, manumitted, and married by the same man. Most of the others were bought by one man and given to another who then married and manumitted her.

It is interesting to note that this practice remained well into the second half of the nineteenth century, for the Khedive Ismail (deposed in 1879) was wont to marry women from the palace to his pashas, who considered it a great honor, boasting of their alliance with the palace through their wives.

Grandees arranged marriages for their men just as a father would for his sons. Ali Bey al-Kabir visited Khalil Bulghia accompanied by two of his amirs and asked for the hand of Khalil's sister for one of his men. Khalil accepted; but when Ali Bey asked him for the hand of his daughter for the other man, Khalil politely refused. When pressed by Ali Bey, he said, "I will be ruined: I cannot afford to marry off two at the same time." Ali Bey then promised to help him financially, and the father gave his consent.[26]

According to Jabarti, our prime source on the social history of the period, the marriage of a mamluk woman was of interest to the entire household. When Ali Bey al-Kabir organized the marriage of Hanim, the daughter of his patron (Ibrahim Katkhoda, the early duumvir), to Ismail Bey, Ali's *khazindar*, the ceremony was of concern to all the beys who had belonged to Ibrahim Katkhoda. Neighboring grandees hung lights on their houses, played music, and offered sumptuous banquets. The celebrations lasted an entire month, during which the gates of Cairo were left open night and day, to allow all who wished to enter the city and participate in the celebrations. At the end of the month the bride was carried to the groom's house in a procession that crossed through the center of town, while horse races and fireworks entertained the populace. "Each amir invested by Ibrahim Katkhoda considered himself a host in that wedding, for the bride was the daughter of their deceased patron." They all accompanied the wedding procession, the bride carried in an *araba* (carriage), while beside her walked Muhammad Bey Abu-l Dhahab, Ali Bey's treasurer (and soon to become successor), carrying a staff in his hand. Behind them came the lesser mamluks, wearing chain mail, carrying bows and arrows, and brandishing long pikes. Turkish music and trumpets enlivened the procession.[27]

This was not the sole case of such a sumptuous wedding at which all the grandees collectively acted as the father of the bride. The importance of such unions was that they cemented a political as well as an economic alliance, to say nothing of the legal one. For men who knew few family relationships, save those within a mamluk household, any alliance represented a link of stability or continuity and family closeness. Recreating family bonds within a household was a conscious action on the part of the patron and his retainers. The initial bond of owner/slave was reinforced by a paternal attitude on the owner's part toward his "sons." He attempted to place them in some position of authority once they were manumitted, to marry them off successfully within his household or among households belonging to his allies and former "brothers." Indeed, the head of the household acted in precisely the same fashion as a father would toward his sons. At the same time the clients behaved in a filial manner toward their patron, espoused his interests and those of his family, and behaved toward the rest of the household as they would have toward blood relations.

Treachery to a patron or a brother was viewed in much the same light as treachery within a blood family. One might go so far as to say that patrons and clients had closer bonds than many between fathers and sons, which often involved psychological traumas.

The same close links as those between patron and client also existed among the women. The slave woman may have looked upon a former owner as a father, unless the relationship had changed and she had become his concubine or wife. Otherwise the bond remained so close that a former slave woman would include the former owner in her will if she had no children. Mamluk women could also own slaves. Nafisa Khatun was said to have married off her slave women to most of the grandee households; this extensive network might explain her vast influence. Networking among mamluk women must have been as extensive, if not more so, than networking among mamluk households. Many of these women had been imported into the country by the same slave dealer and may have developed bonds of friendship while waiting to be sold. Others were bought by the same grandee and became members of the same harem, which would induce friendships and perhaps enmities as well. When in trouble mamluk wives and women appealed to Nafisa Khatun, which shows that the bonds between these women lasted, especially since most of them had at one time been her slaves.

Mamluk women, whether former slaves or daughters of grandees (who technically were freeborn but are included here among the mamluks), were often wealthy through inheritance or self-generated wealth. Some of the women produced offspring who profited from having a rich mother, even when they were unable to inherit their father's position. The husbands of women who had no offspring could benefit through borrowing from a rich wife, who had ready cash (in short supply among the men), or through the advantages of having a rich wife: luxurious housing, a more comfortable life, and fewer demands on the man's income to buy his wife luxuries. Some wives may even have given their husbands property in return for being left a free hand to manage the rest of their assets, for we sometimes see deeds where wives ceded property to husbands. But the most important aspect was the power that wealth gave the holder: power to rise in the hierarchy and to buy supporters and weapons.

Fathers married a daughter to a husband who would look after her wealth and protect her from exploitation, to ensure the necessary funds to keep up the standing of the household, or to cement an alliance with a potentially powerful individual. This was also the standard manner of marriage among the wealthy and the titled in European society. It is not unusual in the modern world for rich men to seek to marry their daughters to their next in command as some guarantee of continuity for their life's work or for rich men to marry their children to other rich men whose property complements their own. Marrying the boss's daughter is fairly common. The mamluks thought along these same lines.

While the chroniclers are silent on the subject, some of the marriages may well have been love matches, as in the case of Muhammad Bey, who divorced his wife to marry her stepmother. The cynical, of course, might note that the stepmother may have been richer than the stepdaughter, having inherited from two dead husbands. However, when a bey married one of his concubines after manumitting her, even before she had borne him children, as often happened, love was probably the motive force. Although manumission of slaves was an act of virtue prized among Muslims, this was usually set out in a person's will and carried out after his death.

These stories lead to certain conclusions. Where the rest of the rural and urban population allegedly prized virginity in unmarried women (although they married divorcees and widows as well, especially when they were property owners), this was not such a premium among the mamluks. They would just as happily marry someone else's concubine, a widow, or a divorced older woman. While the rest of society followed the religious injunction to marry among equals, the mamluks may have looked upon slave women as their equals, for they were former slaves themselves. More important than marriage between equals was marriage to heiresses to keep the wealth "within the family"—the mamluk household. While it was customary for the treasurer or the lieutenant to marry his patron's widow, it was equally customary to marry widows of former opponents who had been killed in battle or assassinated.

Jabarti, who was punctilious in his social comments and often judgmental and arrogant in his remarks, pointed out that the faction of the Qazdaghlis married the widows of their defeated opponents and established themselves in their houses.[28] To him this was reprehensible behavior on the part of the mamluks. Yet it seems to have been a time-honored practice, as one way of healing past animosities and of participating in the riches of the widow without having to confiscate them. Jabarti's disapproval may have been because the widows had been married against their wishes, which in legal terms would render the marriage invalid. Worse yet, these may have been minor mamluks who married wives of grandees, thus marriages between nonequals, which would have shocked Jabarti (a large property owner himself) even more than forced marriages.

Because male children did not inherit their fathers' positions within the beylicate, perhaps the fertility of the wife was not as important in mamluk society. Virginity, which was valued in a society in order to make sure that property was inherited by the legal children, may not have mattered as much to the mamluks, for the bulk of the property went to the grandee's successor. Since a man could take more than one wife as well as have concubines he could buy as many virgins as he could afford.

Those among the middle classes who had little or no wealth frequently married widows who had inherited property. The rural and poorer classes who had little wealth to offer or were too poor to consider marrying more than one wife preferred to marry virgins—a trait common to many societies. So while in theory men preferred to marry virgins, in practice economic self-interest was the prime motive behind marriages, although that does not rule out marriages for a variety of other reasons.

Although the mamluks did not rule over Egypt with a gentle hand, at least they had certain recognizable standards of behavior toward women of their stratum which were criticized when infringed. One incident shows that the mamluks on occasion also supported the property rights of women. Ridwan Katkhoda's widow, the daughter of al-Barudi, a famous wealthy merchant, was harassed by her husband's former mamluk.[29] Uthman Bey al-Jirjawi, who was described as a violent man given to acting without thinking, confiscated some of her properties. Rather than going to court, a long-winded and time-consuming affair, the woman complained to the older beys, who tried to persuade Uthman to leave her alone and return her properties. Uthman, who was then chief mamluk, refused to pay any attention to them, so the beys ousted him from his position.

Different reasons can be adduced for such action, but most important is that it was a move to protect property rights. Mamluks constantly feared confiscation of property and dispossession, so they made sure to deed property to their womenfolk or married wealthy women, as in this case, who possessed extensive properties. To confiscate such property would set a dangerous precedent that could affect mamluk wives and daughters in the future. It may be that Uthman was ousted because he was simply tiresome and annoyed his colleagues, but it may also be because he had infringed on the rights of their former patron's wife.

We also have accounts of incidents where women were abused by mamluks, however; at times women were treated gently and at other times they were not. Property rights were more important in turbulent times and had to be preserved and protected. The same principle underlay reaction to an incident that involved an Ottoman punitive expedition.

The Ottomans, angered by the fact that the duumvirs Ibrahim and Murad, who ruled Egypt, had stopped sending the annual tribute for a number of years, sent an expedition in 1786 to punish the grandees. In the process they punished everybody except the grandees, who, using time-honored tactics, simply withdrew with their men and refused to give battle.

The Ottoman military treated Egypt, an Ottoman province, much like a defeated country to be looted and plundered, rather than behaving as a punitive expedition come to right the wrongs inflicted on the population by the mamluk rulers. The Ottoman soldiery abused the population, while Hasan Pasha, who led the expedition, abused the mamluk women. He imprisoned the two wives of Ibrahim Bey and released them only after they had paid a ransom which included all their jewels. The ulama went to the pasha to intercede for the women and to criticize his behavior, but the pasha said, "Let the women pay what their husbands owe the government." When the ulama responded, "Women are weak and one must have pity on them," the pasha retorted that their husbands had despoiled the country for years and wasted the sultan's wealth.[30]

Not content with abusing the legitimate wives of the grandees, Hasan Bey sold all the female slaves, even those who had been manumitted, belonging to Ibrahim and to the other beys in public auction in the very courtyard of Ibrahim's house. The women were sold cheaply to any Turkish soldier who wished to buy.

Hasan Pasha's ire was not only motivated by mamluk disregard for remitting tribute to the Porte, which needed such funds desperately when a war with Russia was looming, but was also probably an expression of his frustration at his inability to defeat the duumvirs, who refused to give battle.

The beys in upper Egypt sent the pasha a letter, saying, "We have not wanted to draw our weapons against you and have left our houses and women in the safekeeping of the sultan's honor, but you have pillaged our goods and our houses, you have molested our wives and the mothers of our children. Such actions are without precedent even among the most impious of people." This insulting letter did not affect Hasan Pasha in the slightest.

Mamluk women may have been respected by the beys and their men up to a point. Their main supporters and helpers in times of crisis were the ulama.

When the pasha sold the mamluk women, the ulama once again rushed to aid the women, pointing out that it was not permissible to sell free women or slave women who had given birth to children. Hasan Pasha paid no attention and even threatened the ulama. During a meeting of the *diwan* he said, "I will seize their [mamluks'] wives, their children, and their houses. Their wives can go and live in *wikalas*. I will sell everything they possess and all the property their wives possess."

The ulama did not allow Hasan Pasha to get away with such acts. Shaikh al-Sadat, head of the most important mystic order, lectured the pasha on his sinful behavior. He gave him such a hard time that the pasha said, "He has burned my heart" (*ahraqa qalbi*, meaning caused him to suffer anguish).

All the mamluk wives who had hidden themselves at the advent of the Ottoman army were finally allowed to return to their homes on condition they revealed where their husbands had hidden their wealth. Those women who did not know (or claimed they did not) were forced to pay a ransom. It was common practice for rich men to hide a portion of their wealth in secret chambers in their houses. The women were almost always privy to these secret chambers. The Ottomans were not being gratuitously vicious by abusing the women, but were hoping that such ill-treatment would make them disgorge hidden wealth.

In spite of such abusive treatment the wives of the beys found means to send money to their husbands in upper Egypt by bribing messengers. The women were even able to correspond continuously with their husbands, which added to the frustrations of the Ottomans, who could neither outwit the mamluk women nor defeat their men in battle.

This incident involving Hasan Pasha revealed a certain standard of behavior toward women in mamluk society and, even more importantly, showed the close relationship between mamluk women and the ulama, who were willing to face Ottoman ire in order to defend the women's rights. This is not to imply that on occasion the mamluks may not have behaved reprehensibly, but the Ottomans' behavior in selling um walads (slave women who had borne their owners' children) and evicting the women from their homes went too far; these women, apart from being mothers of mamluk children, were also property to be protected on principle.

What did the ulama gain from championing these women? Was there an economic link between them, or were the ulama doing so in order to acquire merit in the eyes of the women's husbands?

The ulama protected the women of the elite for several reasons. First, it was incumbent on the ulama as the guardians of religion to see that religious regulations were followed. Hence women were to be protected by any and all males; if their legal male guardians and protectors were not available, then the ulama stood in loco parentis. Ideologically, in purely religious terms ulama were expected to defend the weak, as the ulama informed Hasan Pasha. The fact that the Quran and the *sharia* also gave women certain rights helped to bolster that expectation.

Second, women founded trusts and endowed charities, from which the ulama stood to benefit materially. The *alim* might be named supervisor of a *waqf*, especially of the public (*khairi*) variety, to support certain charities and ulama might be the indirect beneficiaries should the trust specify the support of a mausoleum or a school or some other charity which supplied the ulama, as a group, with income.

Third, women who were married to powerful men could intercede with their husbands in favor of one *alim* or another. Clot Bey wrote in

1840, a time when women were not as involved in the marketplace as they had been in the eighteenth century, that "les femmes . . . exercent une grande influence. Plus d'un évènement politique a eu son ressort caché dans les mystères du harem. . . . L'empire que les femmes exercent sur leur époux est souvent mis à profit. Les dames musulmanes se voient sans obstacle, et c'est dans leurs visites qu'elles se demandent réciproquement, pour leurs époux ou leurs familles, des faveurs que, sûres de l'ascendant dont elles jouissent auprès de leurs maîtres, elles savent bien pouvoir obtenir de leur complaisante soumission."[31] Though Clot may not have known much about harems, the intercessionary power of women was well known in the inner circles of power.

A powerful woman such as Nafisa Khatun, who was acquainted with most of the high ulama, must have played a part in the political life of her two husbands, Ali Bey and Murad Bey, to have merited the praise of Jabarti, who seldom praised anyone. He referred to her as one "whose merit and beautiful qualities are above praise."[32] Whoever ruled over Egypt came into contact with her—and not only in order to extort money from her. The intercessionary function of wives of powerful men is taken for granted in the Middle East to the present day. Appeals to the women of the harem by a criminal or a defeated enemy who sought refuge in a harem were effective. Clot Bey even believed that criminals taken to be hanged were blindfolded in case they encountered a woman on the way to the gibbet who would intercede for the criminal and save his life.[33]

The close links between ulama and mamluk women were therefore based on moral, economic, and political grounds, an alliance based on common interest and on the ulama's role in helping all women. The following chapters show that women of the lesser social strata also appealed to the ulama for justice with some success. The ulama were the natural native leaders of the country, the intermediaries between rulers and ruled, who held the political system together through a multiplicity of functions.

In 1790, a few years after the Ottoman punitive expedition under Qapudan Hasan Jazairli had been recalled to the capital, where the men were needed to fight another war, plague decimated the country. When the grandees belonging to the factions of Murad and Ibrahim (who had escaped to Upper Egypt from the Ottomans) returned to Cairo, they found that a number of their opponents had died (Jabarti claims that twelve *sanjaqs* died), leaving behind widows and orphans and great houses. The returning mamluks "installed themselves in these houses [and] married the widows of the dead amirs."[34]

There was a high rate of attrition among the mamluks; many of them died young, so that their wives frequently had more than one husband, thus accumulating wealth by inheritance as well as through felicitous investment. Women seldom remained unmarried for long, unless they wished to. Nafisa Khatun never married after Murad Bey's death, but that may have been because she was too old by then, probably around forty-five.

Much of the property of the elites was set up in endowments, which increased during the eighteenth century. Daniel Crecelius believes that this was a sign of fear and insecurity. The powerful feared confiscation of property or being forced to pay so-called loans to mamluk or Ottoman rulers, which might impoverish or even bankrupt them, as well as any other calamity arising from uncertain times and chaotic rule. Transforming property into a trust mitigated such abuses, for neither heirs nor rulers could touch the principal. The mamluks themselves favored turning property into trusts and also "used the institution of waqf to legitimize their seizure of the assets of government and/or their rivals"; by the second half of the eighteenth century, "virtually all large endowments of the mamluk sultans, those who had ruled from the thirteenth century until the Ottoman invasion, and the most lucrative waqf of the Ottoman period had come under the control of the Qazdaghli amirs." These trusts were not inviolable: when the mamluk died, his successors could confiscate his property, especially if he had no heirs, as in the case of Muhammad Abu-l Dhahab's trust. Crecelius concludes that "waqf must be seen, along with the iltizam system, as a source of revenue, social prestige and political influence for all classes of Egyptian and Islamic society."[35]

Women were among the largest group to register trusts. As Crecelius notes, "Women were not only submitting a greater number of cases [to courts] relating to some aspect of waqf but were also establishing a significantly higher percentage of the total number of awqaf founded."[36] The reasons were many—avoiding taxes, avoiding death duties in the Maliki school of jurisprudence, where the state was a residual heir,[37] preventing fragmentation of property, and circumventing the Islamic law of inheritance.

Ways of getting round trusts were also invented, one of which was the "exchange" (*istibdal*) of one piece of waqf property in favor of another. Though entailed property could not be sold, it could be rented or exchanged for ninety-nine years, which was tantamount to a sale. Out of 1,361 cases of property listed in the court registers from 1151/1738 to 1189/1774, Hanna has found that 1,033 cases dealt with semialienation and with *istibdal*.[38] Semialienation allowed the owner to keep possession of a house, but the renter got perpetual rights and could rent it out himself or herself and turn those rights into a trust.

Archival documents indicate that mamluk women bought and sold and invested funds on their own. Their investment in wealth and property was a guarantee of security in a system which provided none of the usual guarantees, since these women had no roots in Egyptian society and no family backing upon which to rely. Those who came from merchant families and who were native-born Egyptians naturally had a wealthy family to sustain them, such as Shuwaikar, daughter of al-Barudi, whose merchant father was fabulously wealthy. But marriages between mamluk elites and native women were rare. Mamluk women, whose support system was other mamluk women, relied on wealth, the only edge they possessed. Husbands and masters had short life spans, given the turbulent times in which they lived. Friends could turn into foes. Survival therefore depended on the wealth they could accumulate. Since they already controlled a certain amount of wealth through inheritance or through access to a spouse's secret hoard, they set out to increase it.

We know little about such women. Although documents contain some details about Nafisa Hanum, mostly having to deal with her wealth and her charities, they say nothing about her private life. This is also true of a woman called Salun, who accumulated a tremendous amount of property. It is as though these women had no past and no roots. Like mamluk men, they are all given the surname Abdallah, the surname given to those with unknown fathers. While Jabarti offered rough biographies for the mamluk men because of their political importance, we know next to nothing about the women, except for their property and wealth.

We can, however, make educated guesses about these women's connections outside the household. They invested in real estate, so they must have had connections with people knowledgeable about real estate (for example, the women whose husbands were members of the *mustahfazan* corps, which carried out police functions in the marketplace). They probably also had connections with a number of merchants through their relationships with the ulama. The high ulama had entrée into the harems and were closely allied to the merchants. Thus mamluk women always had ulama as witnesses of deeds of ownership, for that was the imprimatur of legality on their many business transactions.

Where did mamluk women learn to manage finances? We can only speculate. A father could teach his daughter, but where would a slave woman have learned about management of land property, real estate, and trade and commerce? One likely answer is that they learned it from their husbands, who left them to manage the properties when they were away fighting. Perhaps those women who were successful at managing their properties had a flair for it or had efficient agents. They might even have learned from the various local women who visited the harem to offer certain services, such as the *ballana*, who bathed women and was a depilatory expert, or the retailers of clothing and trinkets and others of that ilk. Or they may have been taught by older mamluk women.

Whatever the answer, women by necessity learned how to accumulate and handle wealth. Perhaps the women who left a mark were the ones who had successfully learned to handle wealth, and those that did not disappeared into historical oblivion. It is clear that some mamluk women had entrepreneurial talents and the opportunity to exercise them, while others probably had none and were content with the wealth they already possessed.

Many women could even be described as active entrepreneurs. In the dossiers at the registry office in Cairo, which list endowments and estates of individuals registered in the eighteenth century (specifically from 1163/ 1749 to 1204/1789), 30–40 percent of all these deeds were made out in the name of women. This alone does not prove much. Since all deeds were signed and registered by agents (*wakils*) acting on behalf of the women, we might be tempted to assume that male relatives had a free hand in managing female property, which was sometimes the case. That situation might have been the norm had these propertied women used only one *wakil*: their husband, father, brother, or son. The *wakil* might even have been a crook, who was not related to the woman, but simply suborned two witnesses to attest to a fictitious relationship between him and the female property owner. But what about cases where the female property owner used a number of different agents, only one of whom was related to her? Can we not then assume that these agents were hired by the woman and guided by her?

Moreover, in cases where the property owner belonged to the elite the witnesses to the deed were generally highly respected ulama, who had no family linkages with the trustee and who stood to gain nothing from the transaction, save the gratitude and the esteem of the woman in question. The presence of high ulama when property was being registered certainly served to add weight to the legality of the proceedings and to protect the interests of the trustee, ensuring that all the legal and requisite steps had been taken so that the trust could not be contested in the future. In a sense, the ulama staked their reputation on the legality of the proceedings.

To illustrate that women hired agents or used their slaves as agents in order to register their trusts, we have examples of female entrepreneurs of the late eighteenth century.[39] Many of these women identified themselves as "daughter of Abdallah al-Baida," a euphemism for describing them as white slaves; all those who had unknown fathers were given the patronym Abdallah, while al-Baida distinguished their color. A black slave would be called "daughter of Abdallah al-Sawda," the black.[40]

Perhaps some form of networking arose among these slave women. We sometimes see deeds where one woman sold or bought from another, although this could be by chance. Bonds of friendship may have arisen among the women even when their husbands supported opposing factions. In any case, there were normal bonds of friendship among these women, who visited and entertained on a regular basis. Such networking was concretely expressed in times of stress, as when Nafisa Khatun, the richest woman or the most benevolent, paid the fines imposed on the other women by the French army of occupation. It is true that many of these women had been her slaves, as Jabarti noted ("most of the wives of the [contemporary] amirs are her slave girls"),[41] but they had also married amirs, who were presumably not entirely destitute themselves.

In other deeds made at more or less the same time, chosen purely at random, a large number of women are identified as "daughters of Abdallah al-Baida" who married men of the *mustahfazan* regiment, most of whom are identified as "sons of Abdallah." Since the *mustahfazan* acted as the police force in the capital, including the marketplace, they may have become rich through insider information regarding real estate or commercial transactions. Perhaps their wives were also able to benefit from such knowledge. Mamluk *mustahfazan* who married native women may have benefited from insider information through their relatives in the commercial world.

Saliha Khatun, daughter of Abdallah al-Baida, a freedwoman and wife of Uthman Shurbaji Mustahfazan, died in 1773, leaving the following properties: 1.5/24 share in a house and the same share in another property, a third house, a tenement, a weaving establishment, a fourth house, a large establishment, two shops and a mill plus their appurtenances, a further property, and a courtyard slum.[42]

Khadija Khatun, daughter of Abdallah al-Baida, freedwoman of Ahmad Qarabas, set up a trust fund of 41 gold coins, each one worth 123 *paras*, with the ground rent of a house and five shops dedicated to the holy cities, al-Haramain. The revenue of ten shops with the floors above them was to be spent on five Quran reciters to recite for her soul and the souls of her children, her retainers, her freed slaves, and all dead Muslims. The reciters were to be paid 150 *paras* per month. The rest of the money was to be expended on various charities.[43]

Of some sixty *waqf* documents I consulted made out by mamluk women, the favored form of investment or property for 40 percent was a "place" (*makan*). This could mean either a house for primary or secondary habitation (women sometimes bought a second house into which they moved at different times of the year, as when the dike [*khalij*] was breached in summer) or a locale with one or several floors which was rented out. Many *makan*s were described as containing workshops outfitted with weaving looms and had shops for rent as well. Of these women, 35 percent owned buildings described as houses as dwelling places for themselves or to rent out; 21 percent had tax-farms, while 18 percent owned shops of various kinds. Some of the women owned a tenement (*rab*) or a mill, *hawsh*, *wikala*, bakery, coffee shop, or storage depots.

Sixteen of these documents supply greater details, showing that 31 percent of these sixteen women were supervisors of an endowment, frequently set up by the woman herself or by her husband; 44 percent were tax-farmers, while 44 percent owned other properties. Four out of the sixteen women were married to men in the *mustahfazan* regiment.

Among the many deeds registered I have chosen to detail those of two women in order to illustrate the different kinds of property that were registered. One woman listed movables and personal items. Her heritage showed the kind of household chattels that a relatively affluent woman would possess: twelve pillows, one pouf, two veils, six cushions, three eiderdowns, one mosquito net, a *rumi* rug, fourteen pieces of cloth, one blue bed sheet, eleven long vests (*yalak*), three outer garments (*habara*), two wide trousers (*shintiyan*), and various items of furniture including a Chinese rug and copper utensils weighing 23 *rotls* (each *rotl* worth 18 *paras*), totaling 2,214 *paras*. She owned a black slave worth 11,900 *paras* and jewelry including 14 *mithqals* of pearls (each *mithqal* worth 550 *paras*), totaling 7,700 *paras*; a pair of gold bracelets weighing 27 *mithqals*, totaling 4,859 *paras*; and four gold rings set with colored stones, one with a diamond worth 1,292 *paras*. She also owned a marten fur and two other furs worth 4,000 *paras* and other items of furniture worth 1,426 *paras*, plus sundries.

Her husband's share of the inheritance, which was 50 percent, came to 32,919 *paras*, with her two sons inheriting the remainder in equal shares. Thus, although she seems to have belonged to the lowest elite echelon, her total worth was 65,838 *paras*.[44]

The second example is Salun Khatun, daughter of Abdallah al-Baida, freedwoman and wife (*matuqat wa zawjat*) of Amir Umar Shawish Mustahfazan al-Shaarawi, described as a follower (*tabii*, i.e., client or former slave) of Amir Husain, Katkhoda Mustahfazan. She is one of the best examples of an entrepreneurial woman, for she began with a modest inheritance and parlayed it into a sizable fortune.

In 1187/1773 Salun inherited four contiguous shops from her deceased husband, Umar. Her agent then was registered as Shaikh Zain al-Din Issa, an *alim*. This was the first document of many which listed multiple properties and several agents (*wakils*), only one of whom was her new husband, Ridwan Kashif, a client of Muhammad Bey Abu-l Dhahab who accompanied his master on the Syrian campaign. Her first husband, Umar, may have died during the Syrian campaign or in the coup led by Muhammad Bey Abu-l Dhahab against Ali Bey al-Kabir.

The second document listed in Salun's name showed the cession (*isqat*) of 1.7/24 *qirats* in a tax-farm in the province of Buhaira on the part of Ali Odabasha Azaban and Jawhar Aga in favor of Salun Khatun, represented by her slave, Barakat Aga, in return for the sum of 178,907 *nisf fidda*, to be paid over fourteen and a half years at the rate of 14,934 *nisf fidda* each year.

In 1187/1773–1774 a certain Muhsin Aga ceded 1/12 *qirat* of a tax-farm in the same village as in the previous transaction to Salun, who was represented this time through another agent, Zumurud Aga, clearly a slave, in return for a fee of 2,529 *pataques* (227,610 *nisf fidda*) to be paid over fifteen years at the rate of 14,500 *nisf fidda* every year. This was twice as much as the previous price paid, indicating either that the land was better than the previous lot bought or more likely that the tax-farm was bigger in size, for the *qirat* was merely a percentage of the whole; according to the new price the entire tax-farm would have been worth well over 60,000,000 *nisf fidda*.

That same year, Ahmad Katkhoda Azaban and al-Mas Aga ceded 1/12 *qirat* of a tax-farm in the same village as in the previous two transactions to Salun through her slave, Barakat Aga, and her husband, Ridwan Kashif, who together acted as her agents. The document made it perfectly clear that the money paid and the property bought belonged to the lady: Ridwan handed over a fee of 210,000 *nisf fidda* specified as being "from his wife's money" (*min mal zawjatih*).

We learn from these transactions that Salun had three agents before she remarried; when she married Ridwan a few months after her first husband's death, he became her fourth agent. In the one transaction in which her husband acted as her agent he was accompanied by one of her slaves, Barakat Aga, who presumably kept an eye on the proceedings. In one year Salun bought tax-farms worth 616,517 *nisf fidda*, to be repaid over fifteen years. By the time the entire amount had been paid, the money would have been devalued to only half its original price—although she may not have been aware of that fact when she bought the land. If the previous owners of the tax-farms died in battle, she would not have to pay the remainder unless they had legal heirs. Clearly those who were selling the properties were military men who needed ready cash. Salun bought her land within the same village so as to consolidate her properties; while we cannot tell how much acreage one-fourth *iltizam* was, we at least know what the entire *iltizam* would have cost had she paid the full sum.

These transactions show that, while land was crown domain to be tax farmed, the elites looked upon it as a commodity to be bought and sold (see the next chapter). Legally tax-farmers were only entitled to the usufruct of the land and a piece of *usya* land, as a bonus, but in practice they looked upon a tax-farm as an investment. Salun was not content with investing in tax-farms only, for in a bad year the Nile could impoverish her. Like any canny investor, she diversified her holdings and bought real estate as well.

In 1196/1782 she bought 1/12 *qirat* in a house from the children of Muhammad Mustafa Shawish for the sum of 7,449 *nisf fidda*. It would seem that mamluk women bought part shares in houses for investment purposes only, although each such share had to be utilizable. Thus dwellings were divided lengthwise; architects were frequently attached to the court in order to divide the house into shares or to specify that divisions were unworkable.[45] Here again Salun bought from the heirs of a military man. That year she also bought the usufruct in a *wikala* and in two storehouses or depots (*hasils*), as well as three bakeries, two flour mills, and a tenement in the area of Bulaq owned by the trust of Aisha Shaaban, for the price of 112,500 *nisf fidda* paid through her husband acting as her agent. Such a transaction clearly indicates that Salun had interests in trade and commerce, both retail and wholesale, for goods in a *wikala* were weighed, taxed, bought, stored, and sold in the building. *Hasils* were storage places for the goods until they were sold and contained shops. A *wikala* also doubled as a hotel, for it had stories with rooms which were rented to out-of-town merchants, who could thus keep an eye on their goods stored in the *wikala* and eventually sold there as well. Sometimes mamluk grandees rented *rabs* for their retainers or their freed slaves.[46]

In 1197/1783 Salun ceded the usufruct of a *waqf* of ten *faddans* for a price of 45,000 *nisf fidda*. She might have invested that money the following year when she bought the right to the ground rent of a house in Birkit al-Rahil. That transaction was witnessed by a number of ulama, including Shaikh Muhammad al-Hariri al-Hanafi, Shaikh Ahmad al-Dardir al-Maliki (head of the Maliki school of jurisprudence in Egypt), one of the most prominent ulama of the day, and Shaikh Hasan al-Kafrawi al-Shafii. Ulama from all three of the *madhhabs* in Egypt were thus present during that transaction, showing the importance and social standing of the buyer and that the trust could not be revoked under the terms of any of the three schools of jurisprudence. There are almost no members of the fourth school of jurisprudence (the Hanbali) in Egypt.

Salun continued to accumulate real estate and commercial real estate by buying an old house (*manzil qadim*) and four shops in Darb Zind al-fil from the *waqf* of another mamluk lady, Khadija Khatun Abdallah, whose husband was also in the *mustahfazan*. The buildings were said to be in poor condition and unfit for use, yet Salun paid 29,700 *nisf fidda* for them. She may have bought them simply for the land on which they stood or as a means of helping break the terms of a *waqf*. *Waqf* property could be "exchanged" when it was said to be in poor condition as a means of breaking the binding terms, which otherwise could be neither broken nor revoked.

A few years later, in 1788, Salun bought three shops for 10,170 *paras*. In 1791 she bought two further shops, three *hasils*, and two stories (*tabaqa*) in the area of Bain al-Qasrain for 22,500 *paras*. She also bought 23.5/24 *qirats* in a *gedik* (see Chapter 5 for an explanation of *gediks*) and equipment used for the roasting of coffee in a shop in the area of al-Husainiyya for 6,300 *nisf fidda*. Four years later she bought a half share in the shop of a weigher, as well as equipment used for weighing goods for 8,100 *paras*.

Toward the end of the century she bought a *makan* comprising four shops in the same quarter for 28,800 *nisf fidda* and rented a half share in a property from the head of the Ahmadi brotherhood in return for 3,600 *nisf fidda*, to be paid over a number of years at the rate of 100 *nisf fidda* a year. Her *wakil* in that transaction was identified as Ahmad al-Tawwab. From another woman named Salun, who resided in Medina and who had bought a half share in a field (*ghait*) for the price of 90,000 *nisf fidda*, she bought that field five days later for 92,700 *nisf fidda* to be paid back at the rate of 1,100 *nisf fidda* every year. Her last transactions were the usufruct in a shop for 11,340 *nisf fidda* and a mill for hulling lentils for 8,100 *nisf fidda* (dated 1217/1802).[47]

André Raymond listed Salun's husband Ridwan's transactions as a bakery worth 9,000 *nisf fidda* and a share of 14/24 *qirats* in a building and eleven shops for 55,800 *nisf fidda*. He also bought two shops and three storage places (*makhzan*) for 16,920 *nisf fidda* and 1,800 *nisf fidda*.[48]

A comparison between the two spouses shows clearly that Salun bought many more properties than her husband and for larger sums of money. Where Ridwan bought property worth 83,520 *nisf fidda* over a period of two years, his wife bought commercial property worth almost five times as much, to say nothing of her tax-farms, which brought her total payments for properties to over 1 million *nisf fidda*.

Ridwan may have had other properties which neither Raymond nor I have come across or Salun may simply have been far richer than her husband, which is not at all unusual. In a period of twenty-nine years from 1773 when she inherited four shops as a widow until the last recorded transaction in 1802 she had bought tax-farms, two houses and part interest in two more, fifteen shops, three mills, three bakeries, one *wikala*, one *rab*, five *hasik* with appurtenances above the storage rooms, and the *gedik* and coffee-roasting machinery and the tools for weighing. One can only conclude from these diverse properties that she was involved in a number of commercial ventures and might have also been a partner in trading activities. Throughout her transactions she used five different agents, some her slaves, plus her husband, who was probably too busy fighting somewhere to do much investing himself. Jabarti said that he had been imprisoned by the French and earlier had fought in Syria against the Ottomans.[49]

Jabarti mentioned Salun one or two times and recounted an incident clearly involving her, although he did not mention her by name. French soldiers ransacked the house of Ridwan. Ridwan's wife had previously paid the French a fine of 117,000 *nisf fidda* and stuck a paper on her door, showing that she had paid such a fee. The French soldiers disregarded the paper and searched her house, claiming that she was hiding arms, ammunition, and clothing for the mamluks. While searching the house the French discovered twenty-four pantaloons and items of clothing, plus arms and gunpowder, and dug up a cache of gold coins. They then put her under arrest, confiscated all they found, including the gold, and fined her 360,000 *nisf fidda*. The search was said to have been instigated by her Coptic superintendent (*mubashir*), with whom she had quarreled, who reported her to the French authorities.[50] Clearly the French had been told where to look to find the gold and the rest. This incident may help explain why Salun was not involved in any commercial activity during the French occupation.

Salun's most active years in buying land were 1187–1188/1773–1774. The first was a bad year for agriculture because of a low Nile followed by famine. During that time those owning tax-farms would have derived little or no income from their lands and would have sold them cheaply for ready cash. Once the famine was over the price of land must have soared, as we note from the prices she had to pay in succeeding transactions. Because of the turbulence of the succeeding years Salun might have decided to invest in real estate and in urban property in the capital, where she could keep closer watch on them. This she did from 1782 to 1785, a period of rapid decline in the value of the *para*. Plague, famine, and unrest followed, leading to a drastic devaluation of the coinage, and her economic activities slowed down.

It is possible, even probable, that not all mamluk wives were as enterprising as Salun, but there is no reason to consider her unique among her peers. Salun and the other women listed in Appendix A were not married to military men of the highest ranks, though they were certainly among the elite.

Jabarti's chronicle mentioned the wife of Ibrahim Katkhoda, who was a daughter of a prominent merchant, al-Barudi. Among her many properties (not fully listed) she had a house and a palace (*qasr*), plus another house, to say nothing of her landed property, which included the entire village of al-Shaqa in the province of Gharbiyya.[51] The wife of Ismail Bey (possibly the ubiquitous, much married Hanim) possessed 241.5 *faddans* in the village of Arimun.[52] Amnatullah al-Baida, wife and freedwoman of Abd al-Rahman Katkhoda, financed the erection of a large *wikala* in Bulaq,[53] which is tantamount to building a shopping mall in modern parlance.

Jabarti also wrote about the wife of the duumvir Murad Bey, Nafisa al-Muradiyya, who was rich enough to be fined by both the French, who gouged 12,0000 *riyals* from her, and Muhammad Ali.[54] She owned the *iltizam* of the entire village of Nawiyya, in the Gharbiyya province.[55] When Murad Bey died, she was granted 100,000 *paras* as a monthly allocation, until her husband's position was filled by another grandee, and even the French gave her 140,000 *paras*.

Similar respect was not shown by Muhammad Ali, who called Nafisa Hanim al-Muradiyya to the citadel in 1219/1804 and accused her slave of fomenting trouble with the rebellious mamluks. When Nafisa Hanim berated him for treating her like a common criminal and calling her into his presence, he apologized and asked her to wait in Shaikh al-Suhaimi's house. Once the news spread of her arrest, the chief judge, the *naqib al-ashraf,* Shaikh al-Sadat, and Shaikh al-Amir (the four leading religious dignitaries in the land) interceded on her behalf and pointed out the lack of decorum in the authorities' behavior. Muhammad Ali was forced to allow her to stay in Shaikh al-Sadat's house until his allegations were proved one way or another. Muhammad Ali was trying to extort money from Nafisa Hanim, but she asserted that she had no more funds, only a pile of debts.

Jabarti did not give us the end of the story, but his account shows the high regard in which Nafisa was held by the native elites of the country, the religious establishment.[56] Jabarti, who almost never praised women, said that she was an influential and benevolent women whose word was obeyed (*al-kalima al-nafidha*) and that she was righteous and charitable.[57] Such incidents clearly show that mamluk women had a reputation for controlling or having access to wealth. Along with Nafisa Hanim, Muhammad Ali (much as the Ottoman Jazairli Hasan Pasha had done earlier) tried to arrest the rest of the mamluk wives, many of whom hid among their friends and could not be found.

Women of the alien mamluk elite were not the only ones to manage and possess properties. The registers show that between 35 and 40 percent of all transactions were in the names of women from all social classes, a 10 percent rise from the time of Qait Bey in the late fifteenth century. We have no way of knowing what percentage of the total wealth that represented. But it is clear that even mamluk women—who were enclosed in harems and who were in most cases alien to the country and barely spoke the local language (though some were daughters of grandees, born and bred in Egypt)—had a hand in the financial and commercial life of the country. Using agents of various kinds, they managed to accumulate both rural tax-farms and urban properties.

One major point to remember in comparison with later periods is that some of that property was paid for in cash, but some was paid by installments. There is no hint that the money was borrowed or that anyone had to stand as security in case the women defaulted on such payments. The transactions were straightforward, with a minimum of bureaucracy involved, and the witnesses by their very presence guaranteed that the transactions were legal, correct, and in good faith.

We shall see how that situation changed in time, when transactions become more bureaucratically complex, involving loans from banks and legal securities. Because of these refinements women's share of activity in the marketplace decreased; women became marginalized and their legal personality, in a sense, was denied.

Quite clearly the wealth of women, even of the second echelon among the alien elite, was substantial; but in no way did it reach the magnitude of the wealth of the wives of the grandees or of the grandees themselves. A woman inherited one-half the share of a man from her parents and inherited one-fourth share from a husband if she bore him no children or one-eighth share if she did bear children. But mamluk women frequently had more than one husband, since few mamluks lived to a ripe old age, and therefore could accumulate inheritances. Furthermore a property owner could will up to one-third the total property to anyone (for example, a favorite wife). Or a property owner could turn all the property into a trust and assign his wife as supervisor so that she could control the income of the trust. The most interesting part of this listing of properties is that the investments did not differ in quality from investments made by males. Both male and female invested in the same commodities (land, properties for rent, shops, *wikalas*, *rabs*, storehouses, mills, bakeries, coffee shops, etc.) and also in trade and commerce.

Women of the elite probably made more investments when their husbands were engaged in warfare. First, the men were absent and otherwise occupied, leaving all property in the hands of the women, as the incident with the Ottoman expedition shows. Second, the men were not around to compete with the women in the economic sphere. This is not to imply that women stopped functioning once the men returned, but they presumably had a freer hand when the men were busy elsewhere.

In time, elite women did not continue to invest as much in land, but turned their investments to urban property. The new and rising groups in the rural areas were siphoning off a certain amount of the profits into their own pockets. Unless the tax-farmer was willing to live on the land to keep an eye on things, the absentee landlord, male or female, was likely to be cheated, even by his or her own employees. Thus on one level tax gouging from the villagers increased, but on the other level some villagers with an official capacity responded or retaliated by keeping the profits to themselves through a variety of mechanisms, as we shall see.

When interest in cash crops arose, the only ones who could really control the crops and their harvest were the rural notables, and no absentee landlord could get as much from them as the powerful villagers could. Nonetheless, investment in land was profitable and perhaps less risky than long-distance investments, which faced a variety of dangers even if they brought a higher rate of return. The safest form of investment was to buy houses, shops, depots, parts of *wikala*s, bathhouses, and similar properties, which is what women did, as well as to acquire tax-farms. Women in other social echelons did the same.

To summarize the situation of the elite in the late eighteenth century, the rulers were weak and thus needed to expend more money to buy supporters from among their own and from among the native elites, such as the ulama.[58] Because they did not control the country, they were displaced by new groups of people who siphoned off the funds that the leaders needed. The leaders and the elites in general perforce had to raise taxes on the urban population and the rural population to make up for the lost revenue, which resulted in outbreaks of violence, sometimes aided and abetted by the ulama. Natural disasters added to the chaos of government to worsen conditions for the populace. However, those who did not succumb to the natural disasters became better off, for there were more lands for the peasantry, fewer mamluks, and more available tax-farms.

It is clear that an elite woman played one role socially, that of a wife and mother immured in her harem, but nevertheless had access to the outside world through visits with other harem women and with nonelite women who came to offer services, so that a social network existed beyond the confines of the harem. From Jabarti's accounts of visits paid by ulama to powerful women, it is apparent that the harem was not so cloistered after all. It may well be that the husband's immediate supporters were also introduced into the harem and could see wives and daughters. This would explain the cases in which men asked for a specific woman's hand in marriage. Relations between a husband and wife must have been caring or the women would not have risked danger in order to send their husbands letters and funds during times of war. The men must have trusted their wives in order to leave all their property in their keeping.

As noted, the women of the elite played an economic role in the affairs of the country. They may also have played a political role, either directly by advising their spouses or indirectly by interceding on behalf of one individual or another.

It has been suggested that economic growth generally benefited elite women more than others.[59] But there was little economic growth in the eighteenth century; on the contrary, it was a period of trouble and disaster with a downward economic spiral. Yet it was also a period which benefited women. Thus it may not be economic growth per se that was important so much as the liberty to maneuver—that is, women's relationships with the state apparatus. When women were not constrained economically by having too many competitors for the same goods, or ideologically/ religiously by being prevented from owning and managing property, or institutionally by state institutions which did not recognize their legal existence, then women became part of the marketplace and occupied a position "outside" the household even when they lived "inside" it. As later chapters show, as a result of changing circumstances, institutional constraints were added to ideological constraints. A Muslim society that had accepted the notion that women could freely play a role in the marketplace altered its views as a result of a change in the relationships between government and society and inhibited women from these same actions.

A new element which became more prominent in the nineteenth century but had been introduced in the late eighteenth century was the European need for raw materials as a result of the Industrial Revolution, first in England, then in France. The Ottoman trading system was opening up to allow raw materials to be exported to Europe and to bring Egypt into the world system of trade and commerce. Thus, compared to the previous form of government in Egypt and the subsequent one under Muhammad Ali, the half century was one of turmoil and unrest, with rapid changes disrupting old, recognized ways of doing business.

The nineteenth century, following the disruption of the French occupation of Egypt in 1798, brought an autocratic centralized government, which introduced new technology, sought to industrialize, and redirected trade from its traditional eastern trade routes westward toward Europe. It also introduced new crops, expanded irrigation, and started a process that changed land tenure and the means of agriculture.

It is clear that changes in state systems resulted in social and economic changes for both men and women. Changes in land tenure, in trading patterns, and in the freedom of commerce affected the entire society, but certainly affected nonelite males and women most of all. Most societies valued men's activities more highly than those of women, yet preindustrial societies recognized the rights of women to become breadwinners themselves. The rise of the centralized state and of industrial society, in developing a proletariat, altered the family structure and turned the father, a member of a breadwinning team, into a wage earner, regarded as the most important member of that team. In the process the family in general changed. Elite and bourgeois families, except in rural areas, made women redundant in the productive sense, while allowing them to concentrate on reproduction. That process of state building created a different role for women of the middle and upper classes and pushed them to the periphery of the marketplace.

4

INDIGENOUS ELITES IN THE EIGHTEENTH CENTURY
Ulama and Tujjar

The accepted native leaders of the Egyptians in the eighteenth century were the ulama. Their basic function was to abide by the Quranic injunction "order good and deny evil": to preserve the traditions of Islam and to see that the Muslim community lived in accordance with its spiritual tenets. They were the purveyors of Islam, its moral guardians, and the repository of learning. When power was decentralized, the ulama played a more important role in society than otherwise, for they represented a focus of recognized authority of some importance in the eyes of both rulers and ruled.

While they did not form a priestly caste, they were established in a position of moral and social superiority by virtue of the "word of truth" which they propagated. The Muslim community (*umma*) rested on a shared emotion of oneness, a self-identity, expressed through the all-pervasive character of the law, the *sharia*. The *sharia* legislated public life and directed private action, regulating relations of human beings with God and with one another.

The function of the ulama was to teach and interpret Islam. One group of ulama dedicated itself to the pursuit of religion and education: teachers, scholars, readers of the Quran, reciters of tradition, and prayer leaders, performing all the duties related to mosque and school. The other group interpreted and applied the *sharia*: *qadis*, jurists, muftis, and lawyers, involved in matters of legislation through interpretation of the law. Since the *sharia* had no *stare decisis* (bound by precedence) a certain degree of overlapping occurred in the decisions of the *qadi*, the judge applying the law, and the mufti, the jurisconsult interpreting it.

Abd al-Rahman al-Jabarti, famous *alim* and the leading historian of that period, in his introductory chapter presented a view of Muslim society and a remarkable description of the ulama. According to him, God created humankind in five categories (this was similar to and probably derived from Maqrizi's view, with a minor difference).[1] The first category, the prophets, were sent to reveal the word of God and convert people to the path of righteousness. Justice could only reign with a knowledge of the Book of God and the Traditions (Quran, *sunna,* and *hadith*). Hence the second category, the ulama, the heirs and successors of the prophets. Following in the path of the prophets, the ulama confirmed their teaching and spread their wisdom. They propagated the rules of just behavior and caused humanity to adopt the good and condemn not only what is bad, but even what is tolerated. That is why, Jabarti added, though at times there may be unworthy ulama, as a category ulama represent the "quintessence of God's chosen" because good and evil exist side by side.

The third category consisted of rulers and kings, whose duty it was to exercise justice, establish a rule of equity, provide security for life and property, and bring prosperity. Rulers and kings must know the Book of God and the *sunna* in order to rule with justice and to establish order. Here Jabarti quoted a *hadith*: "Whoever possesses authority of any kind and does not acquit himself of it righteously shall be plunged into hellfire on the day of resurrection."

The fourth category consisted of the middle groups (*awsat al-nas*), who must observe justice in their relationships with one another and offer equitable compensation for any wrong they may have committed. In the final category are those who discipline their passions and live in justice, that is, the rest of the Muslim community. Jabarti summarized his world view by saying that "a kingdom survives if it is ruled by a just ruler even if he be impious, but collapses under an unjust prince even if he be pious. The misfortune of kings lies in their evil conduct; that of a people in disobedience to their leaders; that of the leaders in weakness of direction; and that of the ulama in love of grandeur." Here we note one of the basic fears which plagued Jabarti and his peers: the people's disobedience of their leaders, ulama as well as mamluks. The populace must be kept under control lest it break loose and bring about chaos. That fear surfaced every time there was a popular uprising, for while the ulama themselves may on occasion have incited such uprisings, they were always afraid to lose control of the crowd. Hence the ulama could be counted upon by the rulers to quell civil disobedience, so long as rulers and ulama saw eye to eye or at least could come to some accommodation. However, the ulama were themselves divided: while the high ulama could impose on or side with the rulers, the low ulama were more likely to side with the populace.

The rest of the population agreed with Jabarti in accepting the leadership of the ulama in all matters. No business transaction was conducted without the presence of an alim to give it legality and to see that justice was done. All official documents had to be drawn up in the presence of an *alim*. Ulama were so ubiquitous that economic, social, religious, or even minor daily activities could not be conducted without them. They officiated at weddings, divorces, funerals, and circumcisions and were present at social and political gatherings. They were intermediaries between one ruler and another, between the rulers and the ruled, and between all groups of society and served as emissaries or mediators between enemy factions, holding a sort of court of appeal. Just as women of the elite could save criminals or those on the losing side of a power struggle by offering them sanctuary, so could the ulama. The ulama were powerful in the urban setting, but they were also powerful in the rural setting, where the only voice of authority was the village shaikh or *umda* and the *alim*. The shaikh was the voice of economics and taxation, while the *alim* was the voice of religion and justice who helped settle litigation and conflicts of any kind as well as being the teacher, mentor, and religious authority.

The ulama were in turn divided socially into categories: high ulama with political and economic clout, who were part of the upper ranks of the native Egyptian elite, and low ulama, who were part of the rank and file and catered to the poorer classes of urban society and to the rural populace. Both high and low ulama came from the same social stratum, mostly from rural areas, although there are occasional dynasties of ulama such as the Mahdi family. Becoming an alim was the only outlet of social mobility for native-born Egyptians.

Religious figures were also differentiated into the ulama, who were graduates of institutions of learning (that is, who had book learning), and religious mystics or Sufis, who had intuitive, mystical knowledge. Heads of mystical orders (*shaikhs al-sijada*) earned that position through mystical knowledge or through inheritance plus a certain degree of charisma.

Among the most powerful of the high ulama was the rector of al-Azhar University, who in Egypt held the title *shaikh al-islam* (in the Ottoman capital that title went to the Hanafi grand mufti). Below him in rank came jurisconsults, muftis of the leading schools of jurisprudence. Below them in rank, though not necessarily in reputation, came the heads of the colleges (*riwaq*) of al-Azhar, generally leading scholars. Sometimes prominent scholars who had no administrative position at al-Azhar or any other institution of learning ranked among the high ulama. Shaikh al-Mahdi, a distinguished scholar who had allegedly been born a Christian, for example, was one of the richest and most learned ulama of his day and one of the best connected with the seats of power whether Mamluk, Ottoman, French, or khedival. He founded a dynasty of ulama who were prominent throughout the next centuries, including one who became shaikh al-Azhar and one who became chief mufti.

Two men stood out among the Sufi dignitaries: Shaikh al-Sijada al-Bakriyya and Shaikh al-Sijada al-Wafaiyya, the heads of the two most popular mystical orders, the Bakriyya and the Wafaiyya. They also alternated in the official position of leaders of all the shaikhs of the Sufi orders (*shaikh mashayikh al-turuq al-sufiya*), for the Ottomans had organized all the Sufi orders, setting up a shaikh of shaikhs to administer them and to sit on the diwans or official councils.

Since the heads of Sufi orders had great, if not absolute, authority over their members, who included most able-bodied men and many women, they could call upon the loyalty of most Muslim adults in the city. Their potential power was very great, as was their wealth. Shaikh Muhammad Abu-l Anwar al-Sadat (died 1229/1813–1814) was head of the Wafai order of Sufis and owned three *wikalas*, which only the richest could afford to buy. One such *wikala* was a three-story building comprising various shops worth 450,000 *paras* in 1207/1792.[2]

Much of ulama wealth in general was derived from the supervision of *awqaf*. Shaikh al-Sadat, who was counted among the richest of his time, was *nazir* over fifty-two *awqaf*.[3] He was the one who could criticize the Ottoman Jazairli Pasha (see Chapter 3 above) for his illegal acts in selling Ibrahim Bey's harem. Sadat also became a thorn in Bonaparte's side when he invaded Egypt.

Shaikh Muhammad al-Bakri, who was head of the rival Sufi order, the Bakriyya, had been a rich man even before he became head of the order. A *waqfiyya* he drew up in 1193/1779 showed that he owned fifteen shops, a vinegar distillery, bakeries, mills, *rabs*, *makans*, a coffee house, and other properties.[4] His assets after he became head of the order as well as marshal of the notables (*naqib al-ashraf*) in 1793 came to 1,151,439 *paras* (see below).[5] He was also superintendent over forty-four *awqaf*.[6]

A third individual who could rank among the religious dignitaries by virtue of his position, rather than scholarly or mystical knowledge, was the marshal of the notables. He was in charge of all matters concerning the descendants of the Prophet (the ashraf), who formed the notability of Islam, and maintained a register in which he inscribed their births and deaths. He also distributed whatever endowed money they had coming to them, for charitable people often left endowments in favor of the Prophet's descendants. The position was frequently held by either a Shaikh al-Bakri or a Shaikh al-Sadat, for both families were among the descendants of the Prophet.

Ordinary ulama were supported by endowments, which financed ulama and students at institutions of learning or paid ulama for presiding at certain ceremonies, such as prayer readings, funerals, and weddings. The high ulama received gifts from the mamluks and the elites. Rare were those ulama who made money by writing.

Most of the prominent ulama came from a rural background, as indicated by their last names and by their biographies. The majority of the population lived in the rural areas, so it stands to reason that more ulama should come from there. Urban people could become artisans or merchants, as did some of the rural inhabitants; but the majority of rural people were either peasants or ulama. The village of Idwa,[7] for instance, supplied several prominent ulama over time, all called Shaikh al-Idwi, but not all necessarily related. Not a single Cairene was elected rector of al-Azhar until the nineteenth century. Some ulama came from an artisanal or mercantile background and practiced both professions simultaneously, as did Shaikh al-Saati, a watchmaker, though that was rare.

The mamluks granted most of the high ulama monthly salaries drawn on the regiments, for each regiment had certain tax-farms to defray regimental expenses and pay salaries. The salaries to the ulama were paid in perpetuity, incorporated into trusts, and willed to heirs; for example, Shaikh Muhammad al-Bakri included in his will a list of 175 *uthmanis* (each *uthmani* worth 10 *medins*) from the *mustahfazan*, 145 *uthmanis* from the *shawushan*, and 72 *uthmanis* from the *mutafarriqa* regiments, plus 170 *uthmanis* from Daftar al-Aytam or the register of orphans, and 100 *uthmanis* from the *waqf* of the Holy Cities, a total of 6,620 *paras* or *medins* monthly. Likewise ulama were given assignments (*cirayat*) from the imperial granary of 1 *ardab* (5.44 imperial bushels) of wheat and 1 of barley, the daily rations of a soldier. The salaries, along with their various fees and gifts, supplied the cash that allowed the ulama to invest in land and other commodities.[8]

In the late eighteenth century the *waqf* of the Holy Cities paid the rector of al-Azhar 19,870 paras, while Shaikh al-Bakri got 260,000 *paras*, Shaikh al-Sadat 148,635 *paras*, the *naqib al-ashraf* 165,291 *paras*, and Shaikh al-Mahdi 225,064 *paras*.[9]

While anyone could set up a *waqf* or could grant the supervision of a *waqf* to a high *alim*, it was the mamluks who made it possible for the ulama to supervise royal *awqaf* (*awqaf sultaniyya*) and *awqaf* with defunct heirs. The advantage of supervising a *waqf* was that the supervisor received a fee for this service and disbursed the funds accruing from the trust at his or her discretion, unless the distribution of such funds was clearly specified in the endowment deeds. Thus the supervision of trusts was a source of riches, especially when the beneficiaries of a trust had died out and the supervisor could dispense the revenues at will. Men as well as women endowed *awqaf*, and all of them used ulama as witnesses for their endowments or their deeds concerning the buying and selling of property.

Further fringe benefits came in the shape of fur pelisses, sometimes sent from the imperial capital, bags of coffee, and other gifts. Even lesser ulama received benefits. An *alim* also received preferential treatment in shops. Sometimes the merchants would refuse payment, considering themselves amply rewarded if the *alim* gave them his blessing. Gifts of clothing and food were invariably made to all ulama, high or low, by their constituents.

The ulama, therefore, while not employed in a money-making profession, did have opportunities to amass riches and were quite successful. The high ulama, save for an unusual few, invariably became rich.

In return for their patronage, the ulama rendered the mamluks service by acting as intermediaries and negotiators between rival factions or between the rulers and the population. The mamluks could not afford to alienate the ulama, who gave them legitimacy and who could mobilize the masses, and granted them salaries and properties. The ulama tried to restrain the worse excesses of the mamluks by guiding and advising them, their ultimate duty. Consequently, while the duty of the governors was to maintain law and order, that of the ulama was to assist them through good advice and good offices. Indeed, ulama preferred to be the power behind the throne, rather than to wield political power themselves. Hence, although not feared by the mamluks, the ulama were at least respected and placated. For while the ulama seldom rose in anger, when they did do so the mamluks were forced to listen to them because they influenced public opinion and led the masses. For example, Shaikh al-Shubrawi, rector of al-Azhar, was the only man who could contend with Ali Bey al-Kabir. All the mamluk amirs held al-Shubrawi in deep respect.[10]

Another *alim*, Shaikh Ali al-Saidi, gained notoriety and popularity among the ulama and the masses in 1777 when he cursed Yusif Bey al-Kabir in a most thorough and comprehensive manner: he cursed the bey, the slaver who bought him, the slaver who sold him, and the person who bought him and raised him to the rank of *amir*.[11] Yusif Bey, one of Abu-l Dhahab's mamluks, could not understand how a woman, at her own request, could be divorced from her husband while he was out of the country. One of the ulama said that it was legitimate to do so according to Maliki law and that he was the one responsible for that ruling. The bey threatened to break his head, whereupon Shaikh Ali roundly cursed him. The humiliated bey could not even retaliate, a clear indication of the *alim*'s standing.

The ulama were granted largesse not only by the mamluks but also by the Ottoman administration. Shaikh al-Mahdi had befriended Hasan Jazairli's lieutenant, Ismail Bey, who was later appointed governor of Egypt for a brief period until the duumvirs negotiated their return to power. Ismail Bey had assigned Mahdi to functions at the abattoirs and the mint; when plague devastated the country in 1790, he allowed Mahdi to take all the tax-farms he wished, probably without paying the full price. This made him one of the richest ulama of his time.[12] He and other ulama also received large fees for interceding on behalf of various individuals with the authorities; this was not approved by the rest of the profession, for intercessionary acts were viewed as a moral duty. Jabarti said that Mahdi could have become one of the leading ulama of his day had he not spent so much of his time in gathering wealth.

According to Hanna, houses belonging to the affluent ulama and *tujjar*, who changed dwellings as their fortunes rose or fell, cost between 30,000 and 60,000 *nisf fidda*.[13] Twenty out of a total of twenty-two ulama between 1192/1777 and 1196/1781 owned large houses, while only two of them were listed as owning big houses or palazzi. The bigger houses had more rooms and larger rooms and used expensive construction materials such as marble and painted wood. In 1777 Shaikh al-Sadat had a private mosque built which cost 3,171,450 *nisf fidda*, two-thirds of which went toward the cost of decorating it.[14]

While the high ulama were wealthy and lived a life of ease, becoming politically involved in the affairs of the country and freely intermingling with those who possessed wealth and influence, the low ulama had neither wealth nor influence with the powerful. However, even the lowliest village *alim* had the respect of those around him, for the ulama possessed the "word of God" through their religious knowledge and, as such, were treated as superior beings by those around them. Whether in town or country ulama were frequently called upon to settle quarrels or litigation. Shaikh al-Samaliji was said to have settled all disputes in the town of Tantah, for that was cheaper than going to court.[15] The ulama interceded between different strata of society, educated those who wanted to become literate, and purveyed the teachings of religion. Whatever small services they rendered were remunerated in cash or in kind, much like a village priest in any European parish. Sunni Muslims did not pay a regular tithe, but they did pay *zakat* (a percentage of their possessions) and *sadaqa* (alms), part of which went to the ulama.

The heyday of ulama influence came during the second half of the eighteenth century, when the mamluks needed intermediaries between one faction and the other; the ulama were thus able to develop a greater degree of authority and to participate more fully in the political life of the country.[16] This was also the period of their greatest riches, when they were materially rewarded by the mamluks for their mediatory functions in settling disputes among beys, and of their greatest influence on public events and freedom to lead the community. Once Muhammad Ali came to power, he divested the ulama of their wealth and authority, though they still maintained their moral tutorship of the community of the faithful.

I have dwelt at some length on the position and status of the ulama in order to show their connections with the seats of power and their subsequent accumulation of wealth, some as a consequence of their links with mamluk women who wielded influence by setting up *awqaf* or by interceding with their husbands in favor of ulama. In return the ulama protected the rights of women, for ulama were the constant source of legitimacy and of legality in the country, especially during times of chaos and decentralization. Because of their close links with all strata of society, women as well as men came to them for justice.

The women (wives, sisters, daughters) of the ulama were also among the elite of the indigenous population, sharing in the prestige and status of their spouses and relatives. Many of the wives of the ulama were wealthy in their own right, either because they were canny business women, as was the wife of Shaikh al-Azhar, Shaikh Abdallah al-Sharqawi (1208–1227/1793–1812), or because they were daughters of wealthy ulama or of merchants, with whom the ulama frequently intermarried.

Among the rare women Jabarti mentioned, although not by name, was the wife of Shaikh Sharqawi. He credited her with creating her husband's wealth through her own business acumen. Sharqawi started life as a very poor man, who eventually amassed a little money through the kindness of Syrian merchants who had befriended him and helped him buy his first house when he was still a young *alim*. His wife, who was the daughter of another impoverished shaikh, Ali al-Zaafarani, invested, administered, and increased his wealth. As Sharqawi grew in importance, his wife allegedly kept the money he earned and invested it. According to Jabarti, "He did nothing without consulting her . . . she bought property, real estate, bathhouses, shops."[17]

When Sharqawi died, his *waqf* listed a public bath, seven shops and a depot, plus a house. His landed property included an entire village; 8/24 in another village to which he added 2 more *qirats* and 2 *faddans*; 9/24 in a third village; and land near the city of Bilbais.[18] Some of that land may have been bought once he had become rector and could use his influence to acquire salaries in the regiments, which thus supplied the cash to bid for tax-farms. But, if we are to believe Jabarti, Sharqawi owed much of his property to his wife's business acumen.

Sharqawi's wife, who survived him, tried to turn his tomb into a saintly one, where she could make money from donations left by people who visited the tomb. Jabarti claimed that she and her son gave a *mawlid* (festival) and forcibly tried to drag passersby in to visit the tomb, but they were not too successful in that venture. The attempt to turn Shaikh Sharqawi, an astute politician and a worldly man, into a saint did not find merit or credibility in the eyes of the Cairenes.

Jabarti admired neither Shaikh Sharqawi nor his wife, which may be the reason why he did not name her. But he seldom named women, except those he favored, like Nafisa Khatun. He never mentioned Salun by name, calling her Ridwan's wife, yet he mentioned the name of his grandmother, a woman he admired. The other chroniclers also rarely mentioned women by name, as a sign of respect, since it was considered presumptuous to call them by their given names unless they were famous and could be addressed as Khatun or Hanim, a corruption of the Persian term *khanim*, "my household," a euphemism for wife. Even the registers use the honorifics Khatun or Sitt (mistress), except when they refer to lower social groups, when the woman is referred to as "the female" (*al-hurma*).

Jabarti indirectly informed us that women of the high ulama were wealthy. For example, he mentioned that Shaikh Umar al-Baqli had married the widow of Shaikh Ahmad al-Muqadasi. She was wealthy, which allowed her second husband a life of ease. When she died, he inherited all her property, including a tax-farm she held in a village named Dar al-Baqar. The shaikh bought white slaves and beasts of burden and was remarried to the daughter of Shaikh Mahmud al-Kurdi.

Jabarti was most informative about his own family.[19] He wrote that Zainab, daughter of Qadi Abd al-Rahman al-Juwaini, married Shaikh Ali ibn Shams al-Din Muhammad. The lady possessed properties and houses, according to Jabarti, which she turned into a trust in favor of her stepchildren (presumably she had no children of her own). One of the stepchildren was Jabarti's great-grandfather. Jabarti's great-grandmother, Maryam, also the daughter of a shaikh (Shaikh Muhammad al-Manzali), was a wealthy woman. Maryam owned a house overlooking the Nile.

When it burned down, many objects made of Chinese porcelain, which only the very wealthiest could afford, were destroyed. Maryam then moved to another house she owned in Bulaq, the port of Cairo; she also had a third house in Old Cairo which she used during the flood season. Jabarti added that Maryam was very rich and possessed houses and land which she turned into *awqaf* in favor of his father, Hasan al-Jabarti. Among her properties was a *wikala*, the neighboring shops, and a house near the Akbaghawiyya school. When Maryam's husband died, she married the amir Ali Aga, *bash ikhtiyar* (chief elder) of the regiment of *mutafarriqa*, a rare example of intermarriage between ulama and mamluk strata.

Hasan al-Jabarti, the author's father and a prominent scholar, owned three houses in each of which lived a legitimate wife, plus various concubines and servants. He owned a large number of mamluks, white slaves of both sexes, and black slaves, an indication of great wealth. Hasan al-Jabarti married Ali Aga's daughter by a former marriage; when she died, he married the daughter of Ramadan Shalabi. Hasan also married the daughter of Yusif al-Khashshab, another *alim*. Jabarti informed us that Ali Aga's daughter bought slaves of remarkable beauty, whom she dressed in beautiful clothing and jewels and presented as gifts to her spouse. According to Jabarti, the fact that Hasan contracted several marriages and bought a number of concubines did not cause her feelings of jealousy.

One can perhaps read more than lack of jealousy in such spousal behaviour—distaste for sexual activity and a desire to substitute other women for herself in such a chore. The woman's alleged lack of jealousy may be Jabarti's own interpretation or his vision of the ideal wifely behavior, although probably not entirely so. Nabia Abbott, in her account of two powerful women in Baghdad during the golden age of Abbassi power, noted that both Khaizuran, Caliph Mahdi's wife and Harun al-Rashid's mother, and her niece and daughter-in-law Zubaida were beloved by their husbands. Yet Zubaida thought nothing of buying beautiful slaves and giving them as gifts to her husband, much like Jabarti's relative. Abbott's interpretation is that "the best gift is that which the recipient desires and which hurts the most to give."[20] In spite of such rationalization Zubaida became jealous when Harun paid more attention to some other woman than he did to her, so the relationship was certainly more complex than any pat answer. Harun, who claimed to love Zubaida, also loved several other women simultaneously.

The historiographers of the eighteenth century are most discreet about the affairs of the heart of any strata of society, unlike those of the Abbassi period. However, since it was commonplace among the wealthy to have more than one wife plus concubines and harems were presumably fairly peaceful places (although they may not have been all that peaceful), a wife may not have minded that her husband had other wives, as long as he treated them all with equal kindness. Harem women of the early twentieth century told me that they were not jealous of the other wives; in fact some claimed that the elder wife chose the other wives for her husband. Let us not forget that the notion of marriage being based on romantic love is a modern Western notion and one not current in the eighteenth century. No doubt some partners grew to love one another and some did not, as in any relationship past or present.

Like the high ulama, their female relatives probably accumulated wealth through inheritance and perhaps through wise investments. For example, in 1168/1754 a female member of the Sadat family, Safiyya Khatun, daughter of Jamal al-Din Yusif Abu-l Irshad, Shaikh al-Sijada al-Wafaiyya, left an estate worth 122,957 *paras*. Of this estate 24,367 *paras* were in gold and silver coins; the remainder was the estimated worth of items such as furniture, jewelry, and copper utensils.[21] That was not the total worth of the lady, for she also possessed 14/24 of a *wikala* which comprised sixty-one depots, forty-eight lodgings, and thirty-one shops; 14/24 of a bakery and four depots, a corridor, and four *riwaqs* in the city of Rashid; 14/24 of six shops; and 14/24 of a property (*makan*), also in Rashid, which included a coffee shop, sixteen shops, depots, and appurtenances. These properties were acquired at various times: 12 *qirats* were registered in 1147/1734 and the remaining 2 *qirats* in 1168/1754, some twenty years later. Presumably she bought these properties and did not inherit them, but the deed does not specify this. Such an enormous amount of wealth may have been partly acquired through inheritance, but the rest must have been acquired through her own activities and acumen.

A member of the Bakri family, who was not a daughter of a *shaikh al-sijada*, was Fatima, daughter of Ahmad Shalabi, son of Shaikh Abd al-Khaliq al-Bakri. In 1169/1755 she left an estate of 4.5/24 of two *makans* and two shops listed in a deed dated three years earlier. She also left the same share in a mill, fully equipped to grind wheat, and the same share in two *makans* as well as in a shop next to one of the *makans*.[22]

Just as the high ulama were supposed to set the example of morality and righteousness for the rest of the male population, their women were supposed to set the example for the female population. Occasionally the behavior of both sexes fell far short of public expectation, as Jabarti took pains to point out.

Shaikh al-Bakri's daughter "consorted" (whatever that ambiguous phrase may mean) with the French when they occupied Egypt; when the French evacuated the country, her neck was broken in punishment. One author claimed that she had become Napoleon's mistress, but there is no evidence to substantiate such allegations. It probably arose because Napoleon befriended her father, who was willing to collaborate with the French, unlike his rival Shaikh al-Sadat, who was one of the leading opponents of the French, and she may have adopted French clothing or customs.

The second group of people who formed the local notability were the merchants, estimated by Edmée Jomard to have numbered around four thousand in 1798.[23] While we have records of dynasties of ulama, apart from a few exceptions there were no dynasties of merchants. Names of rich merchant families were seldom repeated in the chronicles for more than two generations. It was riches to rags within two or three generations at most. Among the few exceptions were the Sharaibi family and the Mahruqi family, both mentioned by Jabarti with respect.

The lack of merchant dynasties is partly due to the Muslim laws of inheritance, which specify the legal shares each member of a family must inherit. By the time all debts had been paid (which according to some schools of Muslim jurisprudence had to be done before anyone inherited) and the taxes on the property had been paid before the property was parceled out among the legal heirs, even large estates were greatly diminished, especially if there were a large number of heirs. Unless the heirs had an acute sense of business and could build up the estate anew from their portion of the inheritance, each generation possessed less property than the preceding one, a further argument in favor of trusts which disbursed the revenue but kept the capital intact.

In addition, Muslims were expected to pay 2.5 percent of their capital as *zakat* every year. With commercial losses resulting from unsafe routes (which all routes seem to have been at the time), extortionist taxes, and forced loans periodically imposed by the mamluks when they ran out of funds, plus *zakat* and legal divisions of wealth, concentration of wealth in the hands of a few over many generations was most unusual.

Among the rare exceptions to the normal diminution of inheritance was the Sharaibi family. Upon inheritance, rather than dividing their capital into legal divisions, the Sharaibis simply kept the patrimonial capital intact and substituted shares, with the revenue to be distributed according to the legal laws of inheritance among the family members, much as one would distribute shares or stock today among heirs. The family treasurer provided the various family members with funds for clothing in winter and in summer and gave them stipends according to their needs. The capital remained intact in one holding, to be invested, and only the income was distributed annually. That system probably lasted for some seventy-five years. The custom of dividing shares among the family members ended when "the older members died." Discord was said to divide the descendants, who each demanded their share in the inheritance, and "prosperity left them."[24] The third or fourth generation apparently destroyed the system that had worked well for many years. Sumptuous living presumably also dented the family patrimony. When Qasim al-Sharaibi died in 1735, his estate came to 12,642,372 *paras*. He, like the richest *tujjar*, traded in coffee and spices. Ahmad, Qasim's brother, died in 1759, leaving an estate worth 574,734 *paras*, one-third of which represented the worth of the goods found in his house, such as clothing, furniture, books, and dishes. A few years later his nephew, Hasan Abu Ali, son of Qasim, left 767,299 *paras*; his personal property such as clothing and furniture came to 219,385 *paras*.[25] One can see how two much younger family members had dissipated much of the wealth over two decades.

Most of the wealthy *tujjar* made their money through trade with the Hijaz in coffee, spices, and luxury goods, which came from the Far East or, in the case of coffee, from Moka in Yemen. Toward the middle of the century strong competition came from Antillean coffee, which was cheaper, though not as highly prized, and which flooded not only the European but also the Middle Eastern market. *Tujjar* then began to look for alternative investments in land or in partnerships with rural notables or *fallahin* to produce crops for the export market. Such was the case in the region of Damietta, where the merchants lent the *fallahin* money to grow rice and then sold it abroad. The same was true of sugarcane. Both rice and sugar were luxury items and were even included among the annual tribute to Istanbul. Most *tujjar* traded in more than one commodity; thus a merchant might take wheat to Mecca and return with coffee. Specialization in long-distance trade was only to come in the following century.

The chroniclers of the eighteenth century such as Jabarti, Damurdash, Abd al-Ghani, and Nicola Turc rarely mentioned women of the merchant families—in fact they rarely discussed women at all except in connection with some unusual event. Aside from inheritance matters, Jabarti and Turc occasionally noted some details concerning women of all social strata, but the other two only mentioned women from the world of entertainment or concubines.

Women belonging to respectable families were mentioned circum-spectly. Jabarti wrote concerning the women of the Sharaibi family that they only married within the family, probably to keep the family wealth intact. The women were allegedly seldom allowed to leave their homes save to go to their husbands' homes and to be buried. This was said of so many women that it might well be a formula to denote the respectability of females, something akin to Boston Brahmin women being mentioned in newspapers only when they died.

Sharaibi weddings were celebrated practically in silence and without the customary processions; in fact, their families waited until the guests had gone to the mosque facing the groom's house to pray during the evening then, in the absence of the male guests, conducted the bride to her groom's house. The bride was accompanied by some of the most respectable women and by singers. Once she had reached the groom's house, the gates were closed and festivities were conducted inside the precinct. Sharaibi women were, if we are to believe Jabarti, invisible: never heard, never seen, and never mentioned.[26] Jabarti may simply have assumed this was true out of respect for the family; but in any case the Sharaibi wedding ceremonials he described were a far cry from the celebrations of a mamluk wedding (see

Chapter 3), where the ceremony was conducted with the maximum pomp and circumstance.

With such a discreet attitude toward Sharaibi women we are not likely to be told whether any of them were entrepreneurial, especially since the funds were kept in the hands of the elders. However, in 1187/1773 Fatima Khatun, daughter of Muhammad Dada al-Sharaibi, the real founder of the dynasty's wealth, died and left an estate that included the following items: 3 qirats and a fraction in a house overlooking the Azbakiyya lake and 1 qirat and a fraction each in another house also overlooking the lake, two other houses, a tablkhana (musical band) and its followers, a further six houses, the Sharaibi wikala in the Ghuriyya, and three different bathhouses and two shops.[27] An earlier document dated 1768 listed different properties, showing that some buying and selling had been going on in the intervening years: 5 qirats and some fractions in a house that was held in joint tenancy with others, in Zuwaila; and the same percentage of a qaa in the street of the Jews, a house overlooking the Azbakiyya lake, a house in Khatt al-Juduriyya, a qaa in the al-Muski, three arcades (bawaki) in Khatt al-Juduriyya, land adjoining a house, a makan in Khatt al-Azbakiyya and the shops forming its facade, another house on the shore of the Azbakiyya lake, another house in Khatt al-Juduriyya, and a house in the same street. Clearly the lady had been buying and selling her investments and above all diversifying her holdings.

If all of that wealth was over and above the family patrimony, then she must have been a very wealthy woman. Even if such property formed her share of the Sharaibi wealth, she was still wealthy.

As mentioned above, Sharaibi men preferred to marry women of the family. Thus Muhammad Shurbaji (Muhammad al-Dada's son) married Safiyya. When he died, she married his brother Qasim. Ahmad Shalabi, al-Dada's son, who owned one-sixth the Sharaibi wealth, married his cousin. Muhammad al-Kabir's nephew Ahmad married al-Dada's daughter Fatima.[28] That was a time-honored practice to make sure that the family's patrimony did not go outside the family through marriage to a stranger.

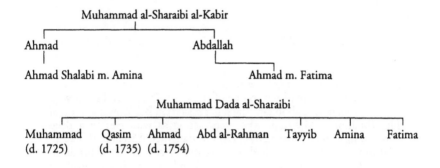

Figure 1. Sharaibi Family Tree

Sharaibi women were also given in marriage to manumitted family slaves (that is, family mamluks, who were regarded as family members). Thus Sulaiman ibn Abdallah, freedman of Ahmad ibn Muhammad al-Dada, married his master's daughter.[29] A few family mamluks, such as Yusif Bey al-Sharaibi and Sulaiman Katkhoda al-Sharaibi, rose in the mamluk hierarchy to become powerful grandees, backed by the family prestige and wealth.

The documents trace the family of al-Mahruqi for at least four generations. The great-grandfather and his descendants were rich and famous under the mamluks, and the great-grandson continued to be equally rich and famous under Muhammad Ali.

We know little about Mahruqi women, save from *waqf* documents. Thus the *waqf* of a daughter of Shaikh Ahmad al-Mahruqi, one of the major merchants of his day, in 1164/1750, supplied the following information:[30]

> In the presence of Shams al-Din Muhammad, son of the deceased Shaikh Ahmad al-Mahruqi, and Haj Ibrahim, son of Haj Ahmad Mirza [Mirza was not an Egyptian name], *sarraf al-surra al-sharifa* [*sarraf* were bankers or money changers; *sarraf al-surra* was the intendant in charge of the funds to be remitted to one of the Holy Cities], and al-Khwaja Shams Muhammad al-Sukari [the sugar maker] in Bab Zuwailah, son of Haj Ibrahim al-Mahruqi, who were acting as witnesses to a deed concerning property owned by (1) Amna, daughter of Shaikh Ahmad al-Mahruqi and his wife, Khadija, daughter of al-Haj Ali al-Jundi al-Qawuqji, who was represented by her husband, Haj Sulaiman, son of the deceased Haj Ahmad Mirza, acting as her legal agent [*wakil*]; (2) Shams al-Din, son of Amna's niece Nafisa, who married Ibrahim Mirza, Sulaiman's nephew, who was his own agent in this deed, and also agent for his cousin [*bint khalatuh*]; (3) Fatima, daughter of Aisha al-Mahruqi and her own cousin, Ahmad al-Mahruqi, who was the *ruznamji* [someone entrusted with recording receipts and disbursements], Amna and her nephew and niece all three together inherited 6 *qirats* in a *waqf* that belonged to Amna's mother's mother's family. Amna, furthermore, inherited a further 12 *qirats* in another ancestral *waqf.*

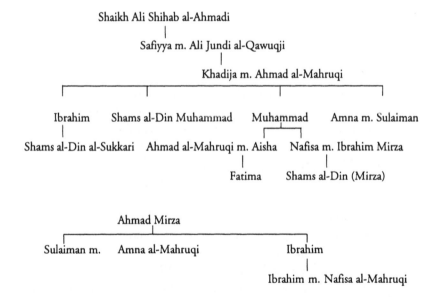

Figure 2. Relationships of the Mahruqi Family

86

This deed reveals the links between *tujjar* and shaikh families. Ahmad al-Mahruqi had married into the shaikh family of al-Qawuqji, who had married into the family of Shaikh Shihab al-Ahmadi, whose wife's ancestors had left the *waqf.*

Amna, the daughter of Ahmad al-Mahruqi, then married Sulaiman, son of Ahmad Mirza, the *sarraf.* Her brother, Muhammad al-Mahruqi, had two daughters, one of whom, Nafisa, married Sulaiman Mirza's nephew, Ibrahim (that is, she married her father's sister's husband's nephew), and had a son, Shams al-Din. The other sister, Aisha, married her own cousin, Ahmad al-Mahruqi, who was the *ruznamji.* Thus the Mahruqi and Mirza families were linked by marriage over two generations, while Mahruqis also married other Mahruqis. It was quite a common practice, which exists to the present day, that a marriage between members of two families often entailed further marriages between other members of the same families. The two families in question brought together a *sarraf,* a *ruznamji,* a sugar maker, and several *tujjar,* as well as descendants of shaikh and Sufi families.

Sayyid Umar Makram, *naqib al-ashraf,* came from a family of *tujjar* who traded with the Sudan. His cousin and son-in-law, Husain Muhammad "al-Tawil," was a wealthy Asiut merchant. Husain's heirs later married the daughters of another wealthy merchant with connections in the Sudan trade, Muhammad Farghali al-Hilali.[31]

While other merchants may or may not have left dynasties, they left substantial wealth. Murad al-Shuwaikh, who died in 1762, left 6,780,469 *paras.* The Shuwaikh family had intermarried with other famous *tujjar* families, for within two generations they had allied themselves by marriage to four other *tujjar* families. Mahmud Muharram (died 1795) left 15,742,498 *paras,* which in real terms should be devalued by two-thirds as compared to a century earlier, but which nevertheless remained a great sum of money.[32]

Marriage between native Egyptian men, especially those of the elite, and mamluk women was not uncommon. It also happened on occasion that wealthy Egyptian women married mamluk men, even of high ranks. Amir Hasan Bey, nicknamed Suq al-Silah because he lived in that street, was married to a lady known as al-Badawiyya. He was the nephew and slave of his aunt Safiyya, who was a slave to Shaikh Abu al-Mawahib al-Bakri.[33]

The daughter of a merchant, Uthman Hasun, married Abd al-Rahman Bey; Amina al-Shuwaikh married Sulaiman Bey Shaburi; Zainab, daughter of a merchant in the Ghuriyya, Muhammad al-Hilw, married Uthman Bey Zada, son of Yusif Bey al-Jazzar.[34] Earlier in the century similar marriages took place, the most famous being the marriage of Ibrahim Katkhoda and Shuwaikar, daughter of the rich merchant Muhammad al-Barudi. Using his wife's money, Ibrahim was able to rise to become the top grandee in Egypt.[35]

Marriages to former mamluks who did not belong to the military ranks but had been bought as slaves in private households were also possible. Mustafa Gaafar, certainly a premier coffee merchant (*tajir fi-l bunn*) of his time,[36] set up a *waqf* of two buildings (*makan*) in favor of four people: his son, Haj Gaafar; his freedman, Haj Sulaiman ibn Abdallah; his freedwoman and wife, Aisha Khatun bint Abdallah, a Georgian woman; and his other freedwoman and wife, Fathiya Khatun bint Abdallah. When Mustafa Gaafar died, Fathiya married his former mamluk, Haj Sulaiman ibn Abdallah.[37]

At various historic moments women were subjected to different interpretations of religious texts that caused them to modify their own manners and actions. For example, while marriage contracts in the eighteenth century included conditions set by the would-be bride, such conditions diminish in the nineteenth century. Jabarti recounted the tale of a marriage in which the woman, who belonged to the Maliki school of jurisprudence, was allowed to divorce an absent husband.[38] Though this was a common tactic in the seventeenth and eighteenth centuries, it came as a surprise to a mamluk bey who was not familiar with Maliki practices. The bey could not understand how a woman could divorce her husband without supplying any reason that he considered valid. Furthermore, she sued for divorce in her husband's absence. Women suing for divorce were supposed to "prove" that an absent husband had failed to support his wife or, in an unconsummated marriage, had failed to pay the dowry, although this was sometimes a mere formality. The ulama sustained the woman's right to divorce her absent husband according to the Maliki school of law. In the nineteenth century that was not possible.

A somewhat similar case involved Fatima Hanim, daughter of Ridwan Katkhoda. She was married to one of her father's mamluks, a *sancaq*, but the marriage had not yet been consummated. When her husband sent for his wife, asking her to join him in Baghdad, she refused and had the marriage annulled according to the Maliki rite. She then married Ismail Bey.[39]

Both these incidents clearly indicated that women had the right to divorce their husbands; the reasons given by the women demanding divorce or annulment were accepted as valid in the Maliki school, especially when the divorces concerned women belonging to powerful mamluk households or to wealthy *tujjar* households. The following chapter shows how women of other strata resorted to the courts to get rid of unwanted husbands.

Different religious interpretations resulted in different attitudes toward women in various Muslim societies. Thus, when the Ottomans reoccupied Egypt in 1786, they behaved in a manner which the population regarded as reprehensible. Their soldiers molested women in the streets, kidnapped them from the bathhouses, and even broke into houses. Such behavior would have been unheard of in the imperial capital. Although the Ottoman soldiery may have been treating Egypt as conquered territory, they commented on the attitude of Egyptian women, which they regarded as too free, thereby inviting unwanted attention—a familiar argument throughout the ages for harassing women.

The Ottoman officers could not control their own men, so Hasan Pasha decreed that women were not to appear in public. The women paid no attention and went about their business, so the decree had to be modified to exclude those who had a profession or a business of some kind (midwives, cloth dealers, etc.).[40] It would have been difficult to distinguish professional women from nonprofessional women by their dress, so the modified decree was probably a face-saving device on the part of the Ottomans, who could not stop women from going about the marketplace. Cairene women may have been freer in their customs and mores than Ottoman women.[41] Soon the Ottomans sent out a public crier to declare that women who went out in public should be modestly dressed and were not to wear a headgear known as the *qazdaghliyya*, described as a circle of multicolored muslin tipped onto the forehead. This headgear was so widespread that even black slaves wore it. Jabarti did not explain why this offended the Ottomans or why the Ottoman army should interest itself in women's fashions.[42] Perhaps the headgear did not cover the face or much of the hair and was regarded as sexually enticing to the Ottoman soldiery, who had not previously witnessed such outré behavior. Women of the middle classes and the lower classes were not veiled. Elsewhere in the Ottoman Empire they may have been veiled, as Lady Mary Wortley Montagu and other travelers inform us.[43]

Cairene women seemed to have behaved in a daring fashion: some of them played tricks on the Ottoman soldiers, even divesting them of their clothing. Some of the Ottoman soldiery must have been sadistic killers, for seventy women were found dead in the house of Yusif Bey, which was inhabited by Hamamji Oglu, an officer. Jabarti implied that these women were murdered by the Ottomans. Perhaps they were the ones who had played tricks on the soldiers.

When the French army occupied Egypt, some women seemed to have adopted a French way of life. Much to Jabarti's disgust, they adopted French clothing, consorted with the French soldiery and officers, and went unveiled in public. Jabarti claimed that these were women who had been slaves in mamluk houses or who came from what he described as "low life," who normally went unveiled. Yet we know that respectable women of the working classes normally went unveiled (although slave women in mamluk houses, imitating their segregated mistresses, may have been veiled), as the women of the native elite probably did. Jabarti may have been so disapproving of such innovations by the Cairene women that he castigated them as indecent. But in that case why would he bother to describe such women, unless they formerly had been veiled and took to freer French customs with gusto?—after all, he was supposed to be reporting on strange doings, not on the banal. This leads me to suppose that some of these women did indeed come from the strata of the elite. Jabarti also recounts that the former wife of a mamluk amir, Ismail Kashif al-Shami, eventually married an officer named Nicola in the French army. When the French army evacuated Egypt, the woman was killed by her first husband.

General Jacques-François Menou had taken Napoleon's injunction to befriend the native population to heart. He converted to Islam and married the daughter of a bathhouse keeper in the mistaken belief that he was marrying into Egyptian aristocracy because her family were descendants of the Prophet. She wore European clothing and gave rise to great hilarity among the Egyptians when Menou bent down to retrieve her handkerchief. However, since Menou had become a Muslim no violence was offered to the woman. There were probably many similar instances which Jabarti did not bother to single out.

Although there is no evidence as to whether other women adopted French styles of clothing, even in the privacy of their own homes, it would be odd if only two women of the elite in Egypt consorted with the French and only those of the "low life" adopted French clothing, which is what the chroniclers wanted to convey as a face-saving device.

Leaving suppositions aside, we do know that Egyptian women who owned property were always ready to protect their financial interests. For example, affluent women who were tax-farmers joined the notables in appearing before the *diwan* and complaining that the French authorities wished to confiscate their properties.[44] This shows that women, perhaps even of the elite, foreign or indigenous, were not averse to public demonstrations and public appearances when it came to protecting their property. Jabarti's account does not necessarily indicate that wives of grandees appeared at the *diwan*, but it suggests that women tax-farmers demonstrated for their rights—and only women who had capital could become tax-farmers.

After the French evacuated Egypt, internecine fighting broke out between the mamluk factions and the Ottoman army—which also contained two factions, one of Turks and one of Albanians. The conflict spilled over to affect the population. Once again the Ottoman army treated the Egyptian population as a conquered people. Once again the women and other tax-farmers as well as fallahin assembled before the Ottoman governor's house and demonstrated against the Ottoman interdiction against disposing of the produce from their tax-farms.[45] The last time women demonstrated in public to protect their landed property was under Muhammad Ali. It is interesting to note that in these cases the women, not the men, were the ones who demonstrated in the streets in defense of their rights.

Such accounts show that elite native women possessed wealth and property, which they tried to defend. They were capable of demonstrating in public against government injunctions, an attitude very unlike that attributed by Jabarti to the Sharaibi women. In recounting other anecdotes

Jabarti in fact gave a different picture of women. He wrote of women who were capable of physically abusing their husbands and getting away with it,[46] of women cheating on their husbands who were suspected of poisoning them, and of a woman Sufi who dressed like a man and followed a mad Sufi around the city. Typically enough, nothing happened to the man, but the woman was arrested and punished by the authorities. While all of these accounts fall in the realm of anecdotes, they offer a picture of women that is a far cry from the one that the elite historians tried to communicate.

If there was an implicit understanding between mamluk men and women on how to handle property, what kind of an understanding existed between native elites and their wives? Merchants and ulama had no recourse but to follow the dictates of the Quran when it came to inheritances. But what about ulama and merchants who married rich women and lived a life of ease? There was no protest when poor ulama who were not their social equals married wealthy women. A rich widow could marry whom and where she pleased and had the prerogative of supporting a husband in a life of luxury. Only single women suffered the limitations of having to marry social equals. In the same way women of the native elites were free to invest their assets as they wished and had a free hand in the marketplace.

One woman named Nafisa al-Sarraf owned 6/24 shares in two properties, a coffee house and thirteen shops.[47] Fatima, daughter of Haj Ali Khalil, owned shares in a shop, six bakeries, three other shops, and storage houses, as well as shares in another four shops and three stories in a *wikala* and instruments for weighing (*wikalas* charged a fee for weighing goods).[48] What is striking in these cases is the diversity of property owned. I conclude that so long as the appearance of modesty and subservience to the male was preserved these women controlled their own wealth. Their knowledge and involvement in the marketplace depended on their acumen and their networks in the market, which do not seem to have been restricted to males in any way.

In times of crisis, which meant whenever the rulers needed funds, males were taxed and made to pay forced loans, which were never returned by the administration. Women were frequently exempted from these imposts by the mamluks and could compensate for the financial losses incurred by the men through governmental cupidity or through trade losses. Women tended to invest in low-risk ventures, though the profits might also have been low. However, foreign invaders—including the Ottomans as well as the French and later Muhammad Ali—all extorted funds from wealthy women.

In *Islamic Roots of Capitalism*, Peter Gran claims that during the eighteenth century there was a rise in studies of *hadith* as compared to *fiqh*. He asserts that Aristotelian logic, on which *fiqh* is based, was at a low ebb in Egypt during the period in question because it was the logic of the state and of the administration, which were both weak during the late eighteenth century. During this period *hadith* studies flourished, for *hadiths* and the Quran look "favorably on the quest for profit, on commerce, and on production for the market."[49] If that is the case, then ulama clearly encouraged commerce and trade; making a profit or gain (*kasb*) was a good thing, though excessive gain (*iktisab*) was immoral. Such religious justifications for trade, commerce, and the pursuit of gain by permissible means apparently suited the ulama and the *tujjar*. But if *kasb* was legitimate for men, it was equally legitimate for women, who could therefore invest, buy, and sell as sanctioned by religion.

The inheritances include other proof of women's involvement in the marketplace, such as the deed dated 1176/1762 which listed a woman as a partner (*sharika*) with the *bawwab* (porter or gatekeeper) of a *wikala*. The porter was responsible for the security of the place and rented out the shops and lodgings, presenting an accounting to the owners. He also profited from exchanging coins and dividing the charges with the weighers (*qabban*).[50] Other deeds showed women lending their husbands money, which was duly registered in a legal document, and a woman being given property in return for her gold bracelets sold by her husband, who pocketed the money, but gave her a piece of property in exchange.[51]

Often the deeds listed landed property, which by the middle of the century was being used as a commodity, even when legally land belonged to the crown. In a deed dated 1193/1779 Zainab Khatun, daughter of Yusif Shalabi and wife of Muhammad Aga, inherited from her father's *waqf* 7 *qirats* in three pieces of land whose total acreage was 150 *faddans*; then she inherited 7 *qirats* in a piece of land of 520 *faddans*. The inheritance meant that she had the right to the usufruct of these lands for ninety years.[52]

The numbers of depots or shops that women bought were not necessarily an indication that their menfolk carried out trade in the shops; they were simply bought to rent out as an investment, as indeed were shares in houses, *wikalas*, coffee houses, and other such establishments, whether bought by men or women. Out of a sample of forty-five inheritances for indigenous elite women, three were supervisors of trusts, five were tax-farmers (a lesser percentage than among elite mamluk women), five owned houses (some of the buildings described as *makans* may in fact have been residences), seventeen (over 37 percent) owned a total of 114 shops, twenty-six (over 57 percent) owned a total of 39 *makans*, seven owned stories above shops, four owned a total of 76 depots or storage places, four owned *wikalas*, and the rest owned a *rab*, weaving establishments, mills, *hawshes*, movable goods, bakeries, bathhouses, an oil press, a dyeing establishment, stables, and other properties.

Out of a total of 809 transactions by both sexes between 1777 and 1781, Hanna found that 700 (86.5 percent) dealt with houses, 57 (7 percent) dealt with *rabs*, 36 (over 4 percent) dealt with *hawshes*, and the rest dealt with other units.[53]

It would seem that indigenous elites were more interested in owning commercial real estate than other properties. That should come as no surprise considering the close links between members of that social stratum and *tujjar*. Furthermore, it was possible to keep a close watch on one's investment in the city, which would have been impossible in the countryside, unless the tax-farmer came from a rural milieu. Thus urban women were more likely to invest in property they could supervise. Because they came from a commercial milieu or had links with such a milieu they might have taken advantage of opportunities to buy property through networks of friends and relations.

The different kinds of properties bought by the same individual suggest that knowledge of the commerce or trade practiced in the shop in question was not always necessary, except among the working women; the properties were generally rented out, probably through an agent, so that the elite women were mostly *rentières*. This does not militate against some of them being directly involved in commerce, as in the case of women who owned *wikalas*, mills, or coffee establishments. But investing in coffee or a flour mill or a *wikala* did not mean actually running the establishment. To date we have no evidence that they ran the businesses, merely that they invested in them.

Diversification was a feature of almost all the deeds which showed above-average wealth. At earlier times artisans may have bought property within their profession, if only because of limitations set by the *gedik* system (see the following chapter), but by the late eighteenth century people seem to have invested in property of any and every kind, without limitation, then hired guild members to work in their establishments. Thus many of the artisans were wage earners or minor partners with more affluent property owners; unequal partnerships were an established custom in Muslim markets. This change from unequal partnerships where one partner brought capital and the other brought know-how to an arrangement where there was no partnership, simply someone investing capital and hiring employees, implied that many of the old, accepted ways of doing business were being displaced. This allowed a freer economic milieu, as a first step toward more radical economic and professional changes. The number of guilds had diminished from earlier times, so there may have been a cause-and-effect relation with buying property outside one's profession (as opposed to within); or perhaps the artisans were losing their positions and their instruments of production and being displaced by people with money to invest.

To conclude, women of the native elites, indigenous women, and slave women married to rich indigenous men (for only the rich could afford to buy slave women) possessed the same kinds of properties as women of the mamluk elite, though many more of them invested in urban properties than in rural tax-farms. Some of the native women had fortunes that matched those of the foreign mamluk elite women.

These women married into ulama, merchant, and occasionally mamluk families. The highest echelons of merchants and of the ulama were closely allied to the mamluk grandees, visiting their houses and consorting with them socially. In the case of the ulama it must have strained their credibility vis-à-vis the native population to act as intermediaries between the rulers and the ruled when they were so clearly identified, through marriage and common interests, with the rulers. Rich ulama such as Jabarti himself had more in common, economically speaking, with the rich mamluks than with the proletariat. That ambiguity comes across in Jabarti's animosity to the rabble (*ghawgha*) or the people of the bazaar (*suqa*).

Jabarti described merchant and ulama funerals and wedding feasts, which were always attended by the ruling beys. According to Jabarti, the mamluk *amirs* visited certain families of ulama and merchants, such as the Sharaibis, without being invited. This indicates a close degree of friendship and shows that these three sections of society really formed the elite.

We are not told whether the same degree of friendship and common interest existed among the women of these social groups. If it did, then perhaps mamluk women learned about the marketplace and about investing funds in property by consulting with the women of ulama and merchant families.

While close contacts among the mamluks, the higher ranks of the regiments, the merchants, and the high ulama existed throughout the century, they were closer during the first half of the century than during the second half. As pointed out in Chapter 2, the changes Ali Bey al-Kabir wrought in the mamluk system by importing grown men as mercenaries caused the links between the new mamluks and the native population to become weakened. The new mamluks did not adapt to the old system of the mamluks, with a symbiotic relationship between artisans and regiments; consequently they treated the native population in a crude and ruthless fashion. This, of course, explains Jabarti's sour tone when referring to Ali Bey and his men. The grandees, by contrast, were old mamluks, and their links with the population remained. This was not the case among the lower ranks of the mamluks or among their rank and file, save for those who had been born and bred in Egypt.

In one sense this was the beginning of the break between the mamluks and the native population. The previous practice of the common people, the artisans, intermarrying with the rank and file of the military, the regiments, ceased, creating a gulf between the two groups. Furthermore, as the old grandees began to die out and became replaced by younger, less established grandees, the links between the native elite and the foreign elite also diminished. The same thing may have happened among the women.

By the end of the century the *para* was greatly devalued and economic conditions for men and women had deteriorated. The only ones who may not have suffered as much hardship as the rest of the population were the high ulama, who were needed as intermediaries between factions. The more chaotic the ruling institution became, the more the rulers needed the ulama to give them respectability and help control the rest of society. The mamluks also needed the merchants to supplement grandee incomes with partnerships in trade and commerce.

Women of the indigenous merchant elite possessed property, not only through inheritance but through their own efforts. As daughters and wives of merchants, they must have learned about the marketplace from the men. Some of them might even have had a flair for the marketplace. Women of the ulama families would have learned the same thing, for they were closely allied to the merchants. Most merchants mentioned in the deeds were identified as Haj, showing they had performed the pilgrimage and thus were probably religious men. Hence their links with the ulama were forged on several levels, including both religion and common interest. All these groups shared a common culture and world view as well as a common education and ethical system, even when they belonged to religious minorities. The same close relationship was to be found among the artisans, the men of the regiments, and the lesser ulama, as we shall see in the following chapter.

It is the elite merchant and ulama group of women that was to suffer the most in the nineteenth century. Their male relatives lost their positions in society, for the merchants were either coerced or coopted into becoming government officials under Muhammad Ali, who controlled all trade. The only new merchants who flocked to Egypt were foreigners. Under Muhammad Ali most of the trade was with Europe, which had represented only 15 percent of the trade in the past. Thus, Muhammad Ali's policies allowed the Europeans to displace the Egyptian merchants. Some merchants did resurface once trade was left free, including wealthy men who traded in the Hijaz or in the Sudan, such as al-Mahruqi and Hasan Musa al-Aqqad. The ulama likewise lost out, for their salaries from the regiments were canceled, along with the regiments, and their supervisory control of endowments and trust funds came to an end when the ruler took over that function. Muhammad Ali put all public endowments under government control and made the ulama salaried officials. They thus lost not only their main sources of wealth but also much of their standing in society. The new breed of bureaucrats were European educated or at least followed a new system which owed nothing to the ulama. The new secular educational system introduced by Muhammad Ali and expanded by his grandson Ismail ended the ulama's monopoly on education. The ubiquity of the ulama in urban life slowly eroded, and with it their power as protectors and intermediaries.

The last domain of the ulama became the teaching and interpretation of religion, but in this they were acting as government employees and not as authorities with an independent power base and nongovernmental sources of wealth. They could no longer afford to challenge the government administration, for they had become part and parcel of that administration. This meant that their wives and daughters could not inherit as much and could not marry into an equally affluent class of men. It also meant that the expertise these women had acquired was no longer useful to them.

The ulama and their female relatives could no longer participate in the market economy. They lost their standing in society and were pushed into a lower echelon. A very favored few, such as the shaikh al-Azhar, continued to belong to the ranks of the elite, and some ulama sent their sons to the new governmental schools to become government bureaucrats. Others maintained their connections with the elite and were able to acquire properties from the rulers, for even Muhammad Ali was generous to those ulama of whom he approved and granted them salaries and properties, but these were in the minority.

5

ARTISANS AND *AYAN*
Urban and Rural Middle and Lower Classes in the Eighteenth Century

Social divisions were based on wealth, birth, profession, and connections but not entirely on any one of them. Such divisions were not clear-cut, which is why I treat both artisans and peasantry within the same chapter. *Ayan* were rural notables who derived their wealth primarily from agriculture (for example, village chiefs).

We can in fact talk of three different groups among the larger category of artisans. The wealthiest, who qualify for the description "comfortable," but in no way came near the fortunes of the long-distance *tujjar*, were those who pressed sesame oil, made sugar, exchanged currency, or acted as bankers (*sarraf*), weighers (*wazzan*), and contractors (*simsar*).[1] Scribes and accountants employed in the administration also belonged to this stratum, although the top echelon of these professions could be included among the native elites. Affluent peasants (*shaikhs al-balad*) and *umdas* can also be included in this group. In brief, wealth, profession, and connections together determined status, prestige, and social position.

Among the second level, who were moderately comfortable, were those who dealt in the weaving and selling of textiles. Raymond estimated their average inheritances to be around 29,644 *paras*. They not only sold the textiles but were owners of looms (*qaat hiyaka*) and had artisans working for them. The third level were members of professions such as rope maker and carpenter. Their rural counterparts were those peasants who had a small *athariyya* (hereditary usufruct rights to land) or in upper Egypt those who received the poorer soils to till, who lost out when the Nile was low. The fourth level included the poor, the day laborers, and those poorer still, without any visible means of regular support save occasional or seasonal work as wage laborers. Landless peasants could be included in that category.

The division between long-distance *tujjar* and local merchants was quite definite, while the one between comfortably wealthy artisans/merchants and the poor was blurred, especially in the case of less affluent merchants who might be part of the middle stratum and more affluent artisans who not only made goods, but also sold them, such as jewelers and goldsmiths. Jewelers and goldsmiths who might be artisans but also traded in precious stones were often part of the elite stratum. Less affluent artisans and the poor peasants had more in common than either had with the richer artisans. The lower stratum among the middle groups might include poor artisans barely eking out a living, who might even decline into unemployment, as happened among many textile workers when production patterns changed and raw material was exported instead of the finished textiles.

We know little about the people who had never been artisans and were always without recognized employment, although we have more information about those who practiced illegal trades, such as thieves and prostitutes.

Raymond quoted Maqrizi, who divided society into strata. Contrary to Jabarti, Maqrizi placed the alien rulers at the top; then (in no hierarchical order) came the affluent *tujjar,* followed by the retailers, peasants, the learned, ulama, the artisans, and lastly the poor.[2] According to the ulama, this hierarchy should have the ulama at the very top, for, to quote Shaikh Hasan al-Jabarti, the ulama were *khulasat khassat Allah fi khalqih*, the quintessence of God's elite by virtue of the word of God which they diffused, which was the source of their power to influence action.

Every categorization of Muslim populations put the *fallahin* at the very lowest level. But such categorizations also differentiated between trades, classifying some artisans as belonging to respected and respectable trades, while others practiced despicable or low-class trades. Nicolas Turc listed the following among the *dun,* the base or even the vile trades: itinerant sellers (*baya*), porters (*shayyalin*), artisans, donkey boys, grooms, pimps, and prostitutes.[3] One can understand the last two categories described as base, although they did pay their taxes more regularly than others, but why should porters (as in carriers, not gatekeepers), sellers, and artisans be ranked in the same fashion? Was it because they were itinerant, rather than working out of a fixed place, or because they carried out trades other than those they were ostensibly supposed to? Or were they too prone to violence and not as easily controlled by the ulama? The French savants claimed that the *bas peuple*, the "lower orders," used drugs—that two-thirds of the artisans were drugged, while the rest used such products in their homes. They said that there was a guild of "sellers of honeyed hashish balls" and that the coffee houses sold opium.[4] Were these the people regarded as base? Shaikh Hasan al-Hijazi, an *alim*, wrote a poem in which he castigated the "wicked and dirty sellers, who cheat,"[5] but sellers in shops could cheat as much as itinerant sellers, though the *muhtasib*—the public official in charge of public morals and fair dealing in the market place, the consumer advocate of his day—tried to control such practices.

Whatever the reason, there seemed to be some consensus that these itinerant sellers, along with petty traders and that vague description of the *suqa*, the bazaaris and sellers, represented the lowest grouping of urban society, which the more affluent regarded as beyond respectability. Toward the end of the century that grouping grew in size and included artisans who had lost their trades, such as textile weavers.

Mobility from one subgroup of artisans to a lower subgroup was frequent, depending on the economic situation; hence the categorization of both groups within the same stratum. The same could be said of the peasants, who might at one time have owned an established hereditary right to till a certain piece of land and then lost it permanently or temporarily.

The savants of the French expedition to Egypt estimated the total population of artisans at the end of the century at 25,000 artisans and masters and 5,000 sellers, out of a total estimated male population of 90,000;[6] they calculated the number of guilds at 193, of which 74 were manufacturing artisanal guilds, 65 commercial, 39 services, 11 entertainment, and 4 others. Raymond quoted Evliya Celebi, a traveler to Egypt in a much earlier age, as citing 262 guilds.[7] The two figures clearly show a decline in the work force from previous periods, a consequence of the wars, plagues, and famines overwhelming the country in the last two decades of the century.

Beyond a decline in numbers of workers there was a decline in the value of money and consequently a decline in the standard of living as well. In his work on the artisans and merchants of Cairo, André Raymond noted the disparity in fortunes among the individuals he examined. He estimated

Table 2. Ownership of Fortunes Listed in the Inheritances

No. of Men	Percentage of Men	Percentage of Fortunes
17	3	50.15
283	49.91	4.3

the difference between the richest and the poorest to be in a proportion of 1:10, as in comparing the estate of a coffee merchant with that of an oil merchant. Thus 3 percent of the total number of individuals he studied owned 50.15 percent of the total fortunes listed in the inheritances, while 49.91 percent of the estates owned 4.3 percent of the total fortunes

Raymond also estimated that the disparity in fortunes tended to increase during periods of economic crises so that the poor became poorer, the worse period being between 1792 and 1798, when the situation of the artisans reached an all-time low.[8] The average estate for artisans and merchants, estimated at 60,523 in constant paras in 1776–1785, fell to 53,095 *paras* in 1786–1791 and fell even lower to 36,524 *paras* in 1792–1798.[9]

For women of the artisanal class (those whose fathers, husbands, and own activities fit into that stratum, but not including merchants), the average estate between 1765 and 1775 was 13,852 *paras*; between 1780 and 1795 it fell to 9,371 *paras*; and from 1795 and 1805 it fell even lower, to 7,740 *paras* in *paras* of the day (see Table 3),[10] when the constant *para* had declined by 20 percent so that the lowest income was 6,192 in constant *paras*.

Table 3. Average Estates for Men and Women of the Artisanal Class

	Men
1776–1785	60,523 constant *paras*
1786–1791	53,095 constant *paras*
1792–1798	36,524 constant *paras*
	Women
1765–1775	13,852 *paras* of the day
1780–1795	9,371 *paras* of the day
1795–1805	7,740 *paras* of the day
	(6,192 constant *paras*)

There were major crises in 1786, 1791, 1795, 1798, and 1801. The last two decades of the eighteenth century witnessed a series of crises: political upheaval, military occupation, famine, or plague, repeated in almost cyclical fashion, with consequent devastation of the land.

The estates for merchants averaged 808,991 constant *paras* from 1761 to 1780 and 956,738 *paras* from 1781 to 1798.[11] These figures indicate that while the majority of the population was not doing well financially some merchants were doing better than ever, suggesting that commerce was thriving at the expense of artisanal production. Where Raymond read into this comparison an example of a static or gelled (*figée*) society, I see in it the picture of an afflicted (*affligée*) society, cursed with foreign occupations, natural disasters, and an economy that was redirected into a system that encouraged elites to expand commerce at the expense of some artisanal production—a change in pattern of investment, in order to recoup the money lost from tax-farms.

M. de Chabrol estimated the poor to number 15,000 out of an estimated Cairene population of 250,000 in 1801, 6 percent of the whole population. But if the male wage-earning population roughly numbered 90,000, the poor would then comprise 16.6 percent of the males, a clear indication of a decline in living standards.

According to French sources, itinerant sellers such as those who sold fruit and vegetables, drinks of various kinds, licorice, and tamarind earned a miserable living, hardly a living wage. Chabrol claimed that by 1801 a porter was paid 5–12 *paras* a day. By contrast, a worker in the building trade would earn 30 *paras* a day and a carpenter 35.[12] Workers outside the capital earned even less. But, as Raymond pointed out, it is not really feasible to compare salaries or wages paid at different times. If a man whose job was to lay tiles (*balat*) earned 9 *paras* in 1701 and 30 *paras* a century later, one would be tempted to assume a rise in standard of living. But the *para* had fallen to less than half its value in the earlier period, while commodities such as food had doubled in price, indicating a fall in the standard of living rather than the opposite.[13]

Previously the regiments had intermarried with the artisans and protected them from excessive exploitation on the part of the ruling elite. They levied a tax on the successions of the artisans which ranged from 5 to 7 percent depending on the time. But this lasted only through the period in which the regiments controlled Egypt, when the customs was controlled by the Jewish merchants, who had a close relationship with the janissaries. Once the mamluks took over, the situation changed, to the detriment of the weavers. To make matters worse, France, which had previously imported large quantities of Egyptian textiles, passed a law in 1840 limiting imports to textiles of a certain width, which were only produced by new, wider French looms. Thus the ruling elite of Egypt, encouraged by the trade with Europe, preferred to export raw material, on which they could profit more, causing many of the weavers to go out of business.

French merchants, allied with Syrian merchants, also tried to divert the rice export trade from Istanbul to France and caused a riot in Damietta when the population discovered the ultimate destination of the rice. From then on the Syrian merchants dominated the Damiettan rice trade. On the advice of their new Syrian administrators, and with the connivance of Ali Bey and his successor, Muhammad Bey, an illegal trade between French merchants and the Levantine customs officials flourished. For example, in Damietta rice was illegally sold to the French, while European merchants illegally "sold... Languedoc cloth in Damietta without paying the customs charges demanded in Alexandria."[14] While this allowed the city of Damietta to thrive, it also allowed Antoine Qassis, the Greek Catholic customs agent, to benefit even more. In time Qassis fell out with the mamluks and was forced to flee Egypt in 1783.[15] When in power Qassis and the mamluks, not satisfied with the extra income they were making from illegal trade, also illegally taxed the population. A French traveler was moved to remark that the illegal taxes imposed by Murad Bey were more devastating than the famines and plagues that had hit the country.[16]

At the beginning of the century rural tax-farms had been the greatest source of incomes, but by the end of the century the urban tax-farms of Cairo alone provided as much, if not more, tax-income than taxes on all landed property of the time (400 to 500 hundred million *paras*), while the rural tax-farms provided more than 400 million *paras*.[17] This meant that taxes on the urban sector were multiplied far beyond the taxes imposed earlier in the century and also indicated inflation. Either land was not as productive as it might have been, as a consequence of floods, droughts, famines, and epidemics, or many of the resources obtained from land were diverted into private pockets—probably a combination of both.

There was a further reason for the increase in urban taxes and decrease in land taxes. The tax-farm system had been set up to allow the tax-farmer to profit from land by having a piece of *usya* or seigniorial land, tilled by corvée labor, on which crops for the market were grown. The peasant owed the tax-farmer a certain number of days' labor or a certain amount of money. When the price of produce went up, the peasant could pay off this duty faster through cash payments, thus producing fewer commodities for the market and causing a diminution of the tax-farmer's income. The peasants then produced more on their own land and sold or bartered the product in the local markets.[18] Prices were constantly rising from the last third of the century, leading to many internecine feuds between the mamluk houses, who were struggling over control of resources. In 1762 the average price of wheat was 66 *paras*, rising to a high of 79 *paras*; in 1780–1781 the average price was 81 *paras*, the highest price reaching 115 *paras*; three years later the average price was 322 *paras*, the highest price reaching 715 *paras*. For the next ten years the average price of wheat remained in the low to middle range at 100 *paras*, though the highest price was generally 100 *paras* more, save for 1792, when it reached 745 *paras*.

(See Table 4 on following page)

Table 4. Average and Maximum Prices of Wheat in *Nisf* per *Ardab*
(in Constant Currency)

Year	Ave.	Max.	Year	Ave.	Max.	Year	Ave.	Max.	Year	Ave.	Max.
			1695	108	235	1730	63	70	1765	67	120
1661	34	41	6	181	420	1	—	95	6	91	120
2	—	—	7	—	76	2	76	76	7	111	120
3	51	80	8	50	50	3	104	130	8	64	76
4	67	80	9	—	—	4	50	52	9	—	—
1665	—	—	1700	77	105	1735	41	47	1770	—	—
6	—	—	1	41	62	6	53	99	1	—	—
7	—	300	2	74	74	7	41	41	2	155	255
8	95	112	3	57	57	8	51	59	3	152	197
9	—	—	4	56	81	9	49	58	4	131	148
1670	35	35	1705	63	93	1740	40	58	1775	87	117
1	38	46	6	150	218	1	118	143	6	82	82
2	—	—	7	85	136	2	156	156	7	198	198
3	31	35	8	37	50	3	—	—	8	96	111
4	39	48	9	—	—	4	—	—	9	76	99
1675	31	31	1710	24	24	1745	81	112	1780	—	—
6	37	42	1	63	70	6	84	115	1	81	115
7	93	126	2	39	63	7	67	81	2	—	—
8	76	252	3	31	37	8	108	124	3	—	495
9	84	84	4	66	82	9	58	58	4	322	715
1680	30	35	1715	28	33	1750	63	107	1785	352	360
1	25	30	6	53	102	1	—	—	6	315	405
2	—	—	7	60	89	2	76	101	7	106	135
3	88	96	8	87	182	3	58	61	8	158	192
4	78	78	9	70	72	4	47	61	9	—	410
1685	—	—	1720	58	72	1755	77	91	1790	75	86
6	75	75	1	43	66	6	—	—	1	97	254
7	56	78	2	29	106	7	—	—	2	341	745
8	—	—	3	54	82	8	—	—	3	256	342
9	54	117	4	150	240	9	155	155	4	—	—
1690	105	205	1725	60	76	1760	60	60	1795	79	130
1	72	83	6	38	50	1	64	78	6	102	112
2	86	117	7	36	68	2	66	79	7	74	90
3	—	—	8	74	96	3	—	—	8	77	86
4	36	160	9	79	85	4	66	66			

Note: The annual averages were established according to the only information found in the registers of the Mahkama. The maximum prices also take into account the figures given by the chronicles.

Source: André Raymond, *Artisans et commerçants au Caire au XVIIIme siècle*, vol. 1, p. 56.

In 1790–1800 the tax-farmers had to resort to some alternative measures to raise their income: they could produce a single crop for the export market such as rice and sugarcane as many did in Damietta and in middle Egypt or they could sell the tax-farm and invest the money in trade and commerce, especially in the new market that was opening up in Europe. Tax-farmers who needed cash and could not afford to wait, who did not know how to deal with peasants, especially the lesser ranks of the mamluks, who did not have the necessary clout to enforce payment of taxes, or who had small tax-farms not worth the hassle sold them to women, ulama, and merchants. Toward the end of the century, as cash became rarer still, it became commonplace to buy tax-farms on credit, as Salun and Shaikh al-Mahdi did. Whether the full price was ever paid is moot; Jabarti, for one, suspected that it never was.

Because of the political condition of the country and the change in trading patterns, little money was invested productively. Since textile artisans now had to face competition from cheaper goods imported from Europe, a series of local uprisings broke out nearly every decade. Fred Lawson has described that situation as one of "accumulation crises" that eventually led to a "revolutionary situation" pitting the elites against their domestic opponents.[19]

While revolts against the ruling elites were not new to Egypt, they grew more frequent toward the end of the century and involved the ulama, who on occasion incited the artisans to riot. Institutions and elite coalitions that had functioned successfully in the past were now practically nonfunctional. Perhaps that condition rendered a society "static"; it was more likely to create a society in upheaval, where the animosity between rulers and ruled had increased to the level of revolts every few years. The revolts and demonstrations by then had acquired the protonationalist flavor of an alienated populace struggling against alien, oppressive, and exploitative rulers.

Those who invested money in urban properties were not investing in order to create bigger and better businesses. Rather, they were investing in nonproductive but more secure commodities. This is why the sale and buying of houses was the single most frequent investment, as we shall see.

As a general rule, when certain commodities became too highly taxed people stopped producing them and turned to more profitable ones.

Weavers were a case in point. When the price of the raw material rose so that a decent profit could not be made, weavers stopped weaving. Later, when the prices fell, they returned to their trade, as in the nineteenth century.

People avoided flaunting wealth, lest it be taxed, unless they were so rich they did not care how much tax they paid. Most people, when taxed too highly, tried to avoid producing more of a surplus than was necessary to support them, pay their taxes, and set a little aside for a rainy day. There was no point in working harder to amass wealth that would be siphoned off through taxes or forced loans. The exceptions, of course, were investments that promised to yield very high returns, such as long-distance trade, but these were short-term investments in luxury goods that were also nonproductive as far as the local society was concerned—and some even threatened local production. The gap between the very wealthy and the moderately affluent had grown vast in late eighteenth-century Cairo.

Most artisans (though not all), even the pimps and prostitutes, belonged to organized guilds. Each guild was small enough that the head of the guild, the shaikh, knew each individual member and also knew how much profit he had made during the year. The guild was a convenient tax-collecting agency for the government, but it was also a convenient professional organization for the guild members. The members of some guilds tended to join the same Sufi organizations (for example, the members of the butchers' guild all joined the Bayumiyya order). Even the less respectable guilds had connections with Sufi orders and with the poorest ulama, who offered them the same services that the high ulama offered the elites.

To become a part of the artisanal system, one was apprenticed in childhood. Generally fathers took in their sons or, when they had no sons, a close relative, to whom they taught the trade. Women also trained their daughters in their professions such as embroidery, cap making, hairdressing, and beautification, although we have no definite statistics in that regard or any knowledge of their membership in guilds. Once the apprentice had achieved a sufficient level of proficiency he was promoted to the level of journeyman. Some guilds enacted an initiation ceremony for that level of proficiency, while others did not. When the journeyman thought he had attained the rank of a master (*usta*), he was expected to produce an item to be examined by the guild. When the guild members were satisfied that he had mastered the intricacies of their trade, he was inducted into the guild in a ceremony known as the *shadd*. A banquet was given for the guild members; the guild shaikh tied a belt or rope with a series of knots round the waist of the new member of the guild. Since many guilds were closely associated with Sufi fraternities, mystical elements sometimes crept into these ceremonies. In any public ceremonies all the guild members marched in the processions, along with the regiments, carrying the instruments of their trade and the flags of their Sufi order.[20]

Among other factors, Raymond accounted for the poverty of the artisans and lesser merchants by the fact that membership in an artisanal profession was passed from father to son and the artisans as a whole had become hidebound. But artisanal succession from father to son had always existed, in good times and bad, and in countries other than Egypt. One of the major reasons for the poor state of the craft was the demise of artisans in massive quantities, through plague and famine, as well as the survivors' fear of trying anything new lest it be taxed at higher rates. It is true the system of *gediks* had been somewhat of a hindrance in the past, looming large in times of depression, but of little consequence in times of efflorescence. The *gedik* referred to the tools necessary for practicing a trade, although later it came to mean the right to work in specific premises equipped with such tools.[21] A person who had qualified in the guild to become a master and to use such tools had to wait until a slot was granted by the guild members before he could become his own boss and set up shop for himself.[22] Certain guilds restricted their membership so that a would-be master had to wait and serve as a journeyman until someone died before he could set up shop.

By the last decades of the century this was not a problem in Egypt since so many calamities had rapidly diminished the population. Guild members sometimes felt aggrieved when it became possible to acquire a *gedik* through sale, lease, mortgage, or inheritance. Some women invested in buying shops and their appurtenances and tools in order to lease them to a would-be *gedikli*, as did Salun. This shows that a craft was not always passed from father to son. The guilds tried to make certain that those who bought or leased such *gediks* were fully trained members of the profession and not fly-by-night operators who might give the guild a bad name or cause other guild members to become responsible for a shortfall in taxation imposed on the entire guild because of the inability of one member to pay. Otherwise, the *gedik* in the eighteenth century was not a hindrance to artisanal production, especially with the large death rates of artisans during the plagues and famines. It is more likely that so many masters died that journeymen or apprentices took their place when they had not yet acquired the necessary skills, lowering the level of expertise.

Women may have been members of all-female guilds, such as the guild of *ballanat*, who bathed women and offered beautification services, or those who were involved in retail trade and went from harem to harem offering their wares. We have no proof that there were organized female guilds in Egypt, although writers refer to female workers, but we know that they existed in Istanbul, especially for silk-winders, cotton-spinners, and cotton-weavers.[23] Women were also involved in guilds dealing with health care (such as nursing or midwifery), cap making, embroidery, and handkerchief making.[24] The archives contain references to women slave dealers, as in the case of Bahiyya Hanim al-Yasirjiyya, *fi-l raqiq al-abyad* (a dealer in white slaves), who was suing Muhammad Aga Hamza, also a dealer in white slaves.[25] While this reference is to a later period, it clearly shows that women dealt in slaves, suggesting that they may have formed part of the guild system in some capacity, whether formal or informal, although guild membership was not a requirement. In many of the food guilds the women, while not officially belonging to the guild, were the ones who cooked the food that the men sold, so women were at times the real artisans, albeit behind the scenes and not officially affiliated with a guild. Certainly any profession that offered services to women was taught from mother to daughter or to the nearest female relative, just as with the men.

The shaikh of a guild was frequently chosen by the guild members, and the choice was ratified by the administration. It made little sense to impose an unpopular head on a guild since he would not be able to carry out his primary administrative function, which was to collect the taxes from the members. The shaikh had a certain degree of authority, in that he was entrusted with maintaining the standards of the guild, seeing that guild members produced articles that were up to par and punishing guild members who produced shoddy work. He warned first offenders, punished second offenders, and could drum third offenders out of the guild, so they could no longer practice that trade within the guild framework. Some guilds seem to have taken up a collection to help members who had fallen on hard times (e.g., were sick) until they had recovered or even to help set up a new *usta*. The shaikh therefore served as a buffer between the average guild members and the administration and negotiated with the administration to diminish the tax imposed on the guild whenever it became too exorbitant. Then the shaikh would partition the shares of the taxes among the various guild members; hence his need to know how much profit each member had made.

The most powerful and elite guilds were those belonging to the cloth, coffee, and spice trades; one of their heads became the head of all the guilds (*shahbandar al-tujjar*) and served on the *diwan*. They were involved in political events on a more glorified level than street demonstrations, the lot of the rank and file. Guild members usually lived in the same streets, often above their own shops. In many cases the artisans owned their own houses or at least owned part of their dwelling. In her study of habitations in the eighteenth century Hanna notes that half the buyers and sellers of houses came from the middle group of artisans and sellers, representing 64 percent of such transactions, but only 25–36 percent of the total amounts involved. While expensive houses cost between 30,000 and 60,000 *nisf fidda*, cheaper houses cost 2,000 to 3,000 *nisf fidda*, while a house could be bought for even less. Textile merchants were among the more numerous buyers. Out of 57 middling houses from 1777 to 1781, 49 percent went to merchants and artisans who could be listed among the more affluent, while 51 percent were sold to the less affluent.[26] The more affluent also bought 65 percent of the *rabs* (tenement buildings with multiple housing spaces, something like a hotel or condominium). The *rab* could be expensive or cheap, depending on size of the structure and its appurtenances and location.

The late eighteenth century brought an expansion of Cairo to the west; more land for construction became available, yet most of that land went for the construction of more expensive housing. Hanna shows that where modest housing represented 75 percent of all houses in 1678–1682, it was only 54 percent of all houses a century later. Workers who owned a house or even part of a house constituted 24 percent of owners in the earlier century, but had fallen to 15 percent of owners by the later century.[27] Such figures are not difficult to explain, given the number of crises and the devastating results on the less affluent members of society, who did not have a safety cushion to support them.

Among the majority of affluent inhabitants there was a preoccupation with privacy. High walls surrounded the mansions of the wealthy. The houses looked inward, not outward, containing open courtyards with few windows on the streets. Windows were covered with *mashrabiyya* screens to keep out the eyes of the curious, not only to hide the women as many assumed. Only the very poor could not afford the luxury of privacy and led public lives, living in courtyards (*hawsh*es) in which huts for individual families were erected. The various *hawsh*es referred to in the inheritances were large areas filled with huts for the very poor, many of whom were recent rural immigrants. There they lived with their children and livestock, just as the peasants lived in one-room huts which they shared with their families and their livestock.

The streets or quarters (*haras*) in which the artisans dwelt had gates which were closed at sunset. A porter or gatekeeper (*bawwab*) made sure that only those whom he recognized as legitimate dwellers of the street were allowed in after sunset. He was thus responsible for the safety of life and property in the streets. Each *hara* had a shaikh, who collected a fee when people moved into the *hara* and stood guarantor for their good behavior. The function of *shaikh al-hara* exists to this day, even in such affluent areas of Cairo as Garden City and Zamalek.

Many of the lower level of workers lived in what we can only call slums on the outskirts of the cities, as indeed they do today. Workers in trades that were considered dangerous, such as gunpowder, or noxious, such as tanning, were relegated to the outskirts of the city. But there were also poorer people who had no fixed residence, not even a hut in a *hawsh*, who lived in the streets, slept in the mosques when they were not chased away by the guardians, and lived much as do the homeless in urban centers today throughout the world. Such people looked forward to the occasions when mamluks held open house to celebrate a wedding, a promotion, or the advent of a new *wali* from the imperial capital, for then they were fed.

The members of the French expedition described the poorer artisans as dressed in simple blue shirts, living in shacks that cost 10 *paras* a month for rent, and sleeping on mats on the ground with their women and children. They never ate meat, but bought bread and cooked vegetables or eggs. Their women also wore blue shirts, and their children were naked. Only artisans of the higher strata lived in tenements, owned a mattress, one or two pots, and other utensils, and wore better clothes and a muslin or wool shawl wrapped in a turban around a fez.[28]

Other eyewitnesses were less perceptive. E. W. Lane, for example, who lived in Egypt from 1825 to 1828, learned some Arabic, and was generally an astute observer of the social scene, noted that most of the "children under nine or ten years of age have spare limbs and distended abdomens" but did not realize that was a description of malnutrition, for he blithely went on to say, "as they grow up, their forms rapidly improve: in mature age, most of them are remarkably well-proportioned; the men muscular and robust; the women, very beautifully formed and plump; and neither sex is too fat."[29] These were certainly not the ones who had distended abdomens as children, unless in the interim they had managed to obtain better nutrition, which was unlikely.

When Lane described the dress of the Egyptians he noted that many "are so poor as to have no turban, nor even drawers, nor shoes, but only the blue or brown shirt, or merely a few rags." He said nothing further about the urban poor. Lane devoted a small chapter to the "lower orders," the peasants, whose lives were "so simple that, in comparison with the life of the middle and higher classes...it offers but little to our notice."[30] The peasants of Egypt—90 percent of the population or more—rated six pages of description, while "Superstitions and Magic" rated three chapters and some seventy-two pages. Thus are bestsellers made!

Nicolas Turc, who came to Egypt during the French occupation as a spy for the Lebanese Bashir Shihab (who wished to discover French intentions toward Lebanon) and who left a work discussing that occupation, did not describe the Egyptians save to note that the women went around with their faces uncovered and were "possessed" by the French, "sleeping and living in their houses," a source of distress to the Egyptian men and especially to men like Jabarti. Turc also noted the sharp tongues of the Egyptians in general, who were treacherous, perfidious, and duplicitous toward the mamluks.[31] By then the mamluks had been totally discredited as far as the local population was concerned; the umbilical cord that had tied the mamluks to the Egyptians had been severed when their one function, protecting Egypt from invasion, proved useless.

Those at the poorer end of the scale who nonetheless were property owners left an average inheritance of 5,000 constant *paras*, while the more affluent left an average of 50,000 *paras*, and the very affluent 309,230 *paras* for the period between 1776 and 1798.[32] In the case of women the less affluent left an average inheritance of 900 *paras* of the day in 1775 and a high of 32,866—10.7 percent of the male average among the affluent.[33]

For example, a poultry seller (*farrarkhi*) owned a share in three *makans* worth 4,000 *paras* in a total inheritance of 7,925 *paras* (3,883 constant *paras*), a modest estate. Even guild heads did not leave much more. The head of the guild of saddle makers (*surujiyya*) left 9,187 *paras* in 1778 or 5,000 constant *paras*. Among women we find the daughter of a fishmonger (*sammak*) owning 13 *qirats* in a *makan* and movables worth 2,804 *paras*, while the mother of a silk weaver left 4,708 *paras*.[34]

Lane said, "I believe that, in Egypt, women are generally under less restraint than in any other country of the Turkish empire."[35] He and others made the claim that Egyptian women of the "lower orders" flirted and jested with men in public and seldom passed a life of inactivity. He noted that their drudgery sometimes surpassed that of men. They were mostly occupied in preparing the man's meals, fetching water, spinning cotton, linen, or woolen yarn, and making the fuel called "gelleh [*sic*]" and were in much greater subjection to their husbands than women of the superior classes. His remark that women in the towns kept shops and sold bread and vegetables is substantiated by what we know regarding guilds and the lower strata.[36] It may well be that women then, as indeed today, were involved in the informal sector of the economy, which allowed them to earn a living but to pay no taxes at all, since their means of production were unrecognized by the state.

Out of twenty-two deeds of women belonging to the artisanal or middle commercial milieu, only ten cite the trade of both the husband and the father. Only one woman married a man from her father's trade; all the others married men whose trades were far removed from their fathers' trades. In fact, out of a total of eighty-two Qisma Askariyya entries and seventy-four Qisma Arabiyya entries, I have found only fourteen which cited the trade of both the father and the husband, and only two were marriages of people from the same trade.

Based on this evidence, which is certainly neither extensive nor complete, marriages outside the father's trade may have been common-place, although the preference might have gone to a spouse whose trade belonged to the same guild as the father's, especially if the father had no son to inherit his shop and *gedik*. Raymond, however, believed that men within the artisanal group tended to marry women who also came from that group. He found five generations of a family named Murad who were *sandalgiyya* (makers/merchants of satin) between 1740 and 1798 who had all married daughters of dyers. Out of fifty-two estates of artisans where the trade of the father and the sons was known, thirty-five had the same trade, and only seventeen had different trades. Fifteen brothers out of eighteen also practiced the same trade. In nineteen times out of seventy-one an artisan married the daughter of another artisan whose father carried out the same trade.[37]

The discrepancy, if it is such, between the information derived from estates left by men and those left by women may be due to a number of factors. One of the wives of men who married more than one woman may have been the daughter of a man who carried out the same trade, but not all the wives. Or, given the high death rates during the latter half of the century, a woman might have married anyone who was available, whether he was in the same trade as her father or not. It stands to reason that a man would know more about men who worked in the same trade as himself and would opt for one of them as a husband for his daughter, rather than someone outside his immediate circle of acquaintances. Yet, given the predilection for marriage within the agnate or enate circle (the other circle of face-to-face relationships within society), it makes sense to believe that first cousins who married did not necessarily come from the same professional or artisanal groups.

Unless they lived in separate houses of their own women of the less affluent classes did not have the privacy that affluent women enjoyed. When several families lived in the same house some degree of commingling was to be expected, not only among the females, but also among the males. Hanna remarks: "La stricte ségrégation qui était pratiquée pendant certaines périodes dans les grandes résidences de la classe dominante n'est pas apparente dans les maisons moyennes et modestes."[38]

It would have been difficult to carry out strict segregation when three or more families inhabited the same dwelling. Houses, even when turned into a *waqf,* could be subdivided and parts sold off, as we have seen. Within a generation or two perfect strangers probably owned portions of the same house and lived in it together. Such propinquity did raise problems, which were often solved through litigation, as in a case where a man complained that the adult son of another resident in the building was too free in his coming and going, thereby invading the complainant's wife's privacy.[39] A certain amount of intermingling was of necessity acceptable, but only up to a point. Unlike the houses of grandees, which could be self-sufficient (or where the harem had a multitude of servants to do their bidding), houses of the middle and poorer classes were not. Thus the women were forced to go out into the marketplace: "Les éléments qu'on trouve dans la maison moyenne indiquent qu'au contraire, les occupants devaient, pour divers besoins, avour recours à l'extérieur."[40]

Thus notions of private and public space differed among socioeconomic strata. Hanna concludes that the quarter (*hara*) rather than the house became the controlled private space where women could circulate, exchange gossip with other women, and look after the neighborhood children, who all played together. Only the space outside the quarter became the public space for women, where they must be careful.

The fact that working-class women were not veiled is further corroborated by Dr. Abd al-Wahhab Bakr, who cited court *sijils* (records) indicating that even a century earlier women were physically described, showing that they appeared in person in court with their faces uncovered. It is impossible to believe that women were supposed to unveil for identification, then reveil in the presence of the judge, the person who upheld the very principle of veiling for women. One case described a woman as "wheat colored" (*hintiyat al-lawn,* meaning light-skinned), Arab in features, with widely spaced eyebrows, and bearing green tattoo marks on her chin, arms, and hands. Another is described as light-skinned, with widely spaced eyebrows, of medium height, with fine skin. From these descriptions Bakr concluded that women in the seventeenth and eighteenth centuries were unveiled.[41] These remarks cast light on the issue of the Qazdaghliyya headgear (see Chapter 4 above) which outraged the Ottomans, very likely because it left the woman's face uncovered.

The fact that working women did not veil was reinforced by Lane, describing the earlier nineteenth century, who pointed out that women of the lower classes did not hide their faces. Only upper-class women, and those among the bourgeoisie that imitated them, did.

The more interesting detail that Bakr's records revealed was that native Egyptian women frequently went to court in their own right and without being accompanied by an agent (*wakil*), since the documents show that the women were the signatories or fail to mention the presence of a *wakil.* Elite alien women invariably sent a *wakil* in their place, whose name is recorded in the deed. It is very likely that elite women needed a *wakil* not only because they were secluded in harems but also because they did not speak Arabic (the language in which such cases were conducted) well enough to understand what was being said. Egyptian women went to court on issues of inheritance and succession or in cases of buying and selling. In fact, they carried out each and every business transaction by themselves without needing a *wakil* to represent them.[42] The courts before which they appeared were *sharia* courts, presided over by *qadis* from the different schools of jurisprudence. If the women appeared unveiled before these men of religion, there is all the more reason for Bakr to conclude that they must have gone unveiled the rest of the time.

Segregation and the veil were thus the fate of alien elite women and perhaps some of the richest of the indigenous elites and the bourgeoisie as well, who imitated a mamluk lifestyle or who were punctilious about their women, as Jabarti told us regarding the Sharaibi women. It is probably in the middle of the nineteenth century—when the state was becoming more Egyptianized, with more native Egyptians being employed in the administration—that native Egyptian women, imitating their alien elite Ottoman Egyptian sisters, began to be secluded and to wear the veil as a sign that they too had reached the higher echelons of society and belonged to the elite. Since the veil was identified with the elites, it behooved the new Egyptian bureaucrats to dress their women in the same fashion.

Women appeared in court not only in Cairo but in the rest of the empire. Ronald Jennings reports that in the region of Kayseri in Anatolia women initiated suits in the sharia courts. They took oaths in the same way as did the men and were able to defend themselves in court. "Women came to court regularly, freely and openly."[43] Jennings adds that they had the same legal problems as did men, except for those dealing with government, administration, and the guilds. His records from the early seventeenth century and Bakr's records from the late seventeenth century seem to corroborate one another. Court records show that women went to court in the eighteenth and the early nineteenth centuries as well. Women went to the sharia courts because they believed in the system—justifiably so, for often the court gave justice to the weak against the strong and to the women against the men.

Women of the less affluent classes often resorted to the courts to solve cases of personal conflict, including street fights. The practice of exchanging insults in public in rhymed prose (*radh*) existed for centuries and has only disappeared with the present generation. These exchanges offered fixed formulae of insults. One woman might start a litany that would refer to her opponent as a kite with jingle bells, the bottom of a coffee cooker (black with accumulated soot), and the stick of Ali Effendi (meaning she was as shapeless as a stick). The other would offer another set of insults, such as comparing her opponent to Qalaun's wet nurse. Sultan Qalaun was rumored to have sent his soldiers to massacre Egyptians in the street and was known to be a tyrannical ruler. The implication was that his wet nurse fed him fiendish milk, which had no human kindness in it. These insults—much like those Falstaff offered Prince Hal in Shakespeare's play, calling him a "rusted needle"—were updated with every generation. In the mid-twentieth century one of the insults was "Ya photomaton," meaning the woman was worthless (the photomaton was a photographic device that produced ten pictures for a modest sum of money).

Passersby or neighbors in the *hara* were expected to intervene and end the quarrel, but when they could not the women might beat each other and end in court. One woman appeared in court carrying a large vessel used for washing clothes allegedly containing her aborted fetus. She claimed that in a quarrel with another woman she was struck and in consequence aborted.[44]

Litigation was brought by a husband who felt that his new bride's family was making too many visits. The qadi then limited the number of visits made to the bride by her family to one a week. Such visits formed a basic part of social life; one bride inserted in her marriage contract the proviso that her parents and friends could visit her at any time and for as long as they wished, and her husband had to accept that. Such conditions in marriage contracts were prevalent and forcefully expressed. In one contract the woman insisted that her husband could not break faith with her sisters, their husbands, her brothers, and even their followers.

One of the most unusual cases dealt with a woman whose marriage had been arranged by her uncle. After having cohabited with the man for five months, she sued in court, saying that she had never made her uncle her delegate (*wakil*) because she was not a minor so the marriage was invalid. The court accepted her argument and the marriage was dissolved. A woman then obtained a divorce simply by saying that she no longer wanted to live with the husband because she felt unsympathetic toward him, using the legal term *mutadarara*, meaning the relationship resulted in prejudice (*darar*) to herself.[45] That a legal term existed for such grounds is an indication that this was not an isolated case. She too obtained a divorce. In another case the *qadi* ruled that a woman who refused to eat with her husband had to take her meals with him. Other quarrels arose from financial transactions, claims over money lent, or claims of swindling. In one case a woman bought a house and inserted a clause specifying that her husband could live in that house free of rent,[46] since legally he was expected to pay rent as part of his duty to support his wife financially.

Most of the chroniclers seldom mentioned local women except as appendages to famous males (i.e., wives or daughters of ulama and *tujjar*). The few exceptions are mentions of women of ill-repute, particularly when involved in scandalous behavior of some kind. The chronicles of Ahmad al-Damurdash Katkhoda Azaban (*al-Durra al-musana fi akhbar al-kinana*, which covers the early eighteenth century) and Ahmad Shalabi ibn Abd al-Ghani (*Awdah al-isharat fi man tawalla Misr al-Qahira min al-wuzara wa-l bashat*) both mention women of ill-repute. Prostitutes (*khawati*), specifically one named Siqsaqa in the house of al-Nabqa who was married to al-Sayyid Muhammad al-Amwahi, are mentioned along with a famous singer, Al-Anza, described as the chief singer or *shaikhat al-maghani*,[47] which may have meant that she was the head of the guild of singers or merely that she was the best or most prominent singer. Abd al-Ghani mentioned two dancers, Janash al-Jankiyya and Amna al-Jankiyya.

Jabarti, who was something of a prude, described any woman he saw doing something of which he disapproved (such as consorting with French or Ottoman soldiers) as a woman of ill-repute. According to him, virtuous women were neither seen nor heard. Nicolas Turc, however, described the lower classes in Egypt as delighting in freedom: "sellers, porters, donkey boys, artisans, pimps and prostitutes, in brief, the dregs of the population were delighted with the occupation because of the freedom it allowed them."[48]

Deeds made out by women or citing property owned by women do not indicate whether the property was inherited by the woman, whether she had developed it herself, or whether the initial capital came from an inheritance from parents, siblings, or a deceased husband. But some women from all sectors of society were property owners.

The favored form of property for women was houses, just as it was for men, according to Hanna. Out of a total of eighty deeds, 27 percent of the properties listed a house. The next favored investment was in shops (17 percent of the women owned a total of some thirty-nine shops) and stories (*tabaqa*) in some building (owned by 7 percent of the women) associated with a *qaa*, most likely for weaving purposes.[49] As previously stated, shares in houses had to be inhabitable parts of the house or the transaction could not legally take place.

Aside from one deed involving the daughter of a water carrier, none of the artisans or their women mentioned in those deeds came from the lowest rank of the artisans. Those belonging to the lower ranks would be in no condition to leave an inheritance of any kind—they were lucky to be able to feed their families.

In spite of the divisions that separated social strata there were social bridges between them so that no group was sealed off from the other. Elite women were the most isolated. Yet even they had windows on the outside world: they received visits from women of other social ranks who came as petitioners and from women retailers who brought their wares and probably spent a good part of the day showing their goods and haggling for the best prices. Elite women might also receive the weekly visit of a ballana, who came to wash hair, massage, and remove body hair. These women were in great demand during a wedding, for the bride had to be beautified, her feet and hands covered in henna designs, and her hair coiffed. Thus working-class women were a part of the harem scene. While communication between native Egyptian women and elite Turkish-speaking women might have been difficult (although some elite women no doubt also spoke Arabic), the working-class women more often than not learned to speak Turkish in order to communicate with their clientele, as Khan Khalili shopkeepers today have learned to speak Russian and Japanese to communicate with their new clients.

The native women who most frequented the harem were those who had been hired as wet nurses. Healthy peasant women were often brought to nurse the children of elite women. Once a wet nurse was installed in the harem she became a permanent fixture. She was referred to as "mother" by the child she had nursed and her own children who had nursed at the same time became the "sisters and brothers" of the elite children. According to Islam the bond between children who nursed together is so strong that they cannot marry one another, for they became siblings.

The wet nurse therefore became the "dada" or "amma" in the household and her children and husband became clients to be supported, employed, and looked after by their employers. A household with more than one child was likely to employ several wet nurses and their families. Often such connections went on for several generations, with the wet nurse following her "child" into her new home when she got married, and her daughter becoming a wet nurse for her milk sister. This custom remained until well into the twentieth century, when powdered milk and bottles replaced wet nurses.

Among the religious hierarchy *alimat* (in the singular the term can mean both learned women, the female equivalent of ulama, and women of the entertainment business, depending on the context, but the plurals differ: the plural for entertainers is *awalim*) were always welcomed in the harem, along with ulama. *Alimat* taught Quran to the elite women and their children and taught them their religious duties. Frequently *alimat* would be brought to recite Quran to the women of the harem on Fridays. This was also customary during funerals or on feast days or other occasions such as the prayers on the fifteenth of the month of Shaaban (the month preceding Ramadan: *nisf shaaban*), during the month of Ramadan, and certainly during *laylat al-qadr*, the Night of Power, when the Prophet received the Quran.

121

Women of the entertainment business also had entrée to the harem, including women teachers of musical instruments such as the lute (*ud*) or wind instruments, for harem women had to make their own entertainment. Sometimes women who taught embroidery and needlework were also regular visitors, as were women dressmakers and all those involved in the making and sale of items of clothing, perfumes and cosmetics, and jewelry.

Thus women of the middle and working classes did consort with those of the upper groups, both native and alien. Bonds were frequently fashioned between them, and a patron/client relationship consequently evolved. Furthermore, such women sellers formed close links with the maids of the household (*kalfas*) and the other subordinates.

Some rural women also forged links with the city women. The closest links were those between the peasantry associated with a piece of land and the tax-farmer of that land. The *umda*'s wife would probably pay a yearly visit to the harem women on feast days. More importantly, the woman who supplied the *ghee* or *samn* (clarified butter) would come and stay for several days while she prepared the *ghee*, which was stored and sufficed to cover the household needs for the year. The seller of *samn* was welcomed into the household by the lesser retainers, for they could feast on the butter she brought and on the *murta* (leftover salted *ghee*). The household's agent, the harem lady's *wakil*, and her accountant were among the regular male visitors to the harem, for they conferred with the lady and presented their accounts on a regular basis.

Society then was not as discrete as it was to become under the new regime set by Muhammad Ali. Links between the rulers and the ruled existed on an informal basis and created relationships that were used by the poorer classes in times of need. Though such relationships were not institutionalized, they were recognized by society and perhaps lasted much longer than if they had been institutionalized. Under Muhammad Ali these links with the new elite were broken; but they were eventually reestablished, for they exist to the present day in one form or another.

Peasant women also did not hide their faces, although they drew their veils across their mouths when they saw a stranger. Peasant women worked side by side with their husbands in the fields; it would have been impossible to hide their faces while doing manual labor.

In the countryside the disparity between rich and poor was just as vast as in the towns and cities. The tax-farmers held the rural wealth. All land, in theory, was crown domain; neither tax-farmers nor *fallahin* had rights of ownership. Each village was allocated a certain number of acres (which differed from village to village) that only the villagers of that village could till. The acreage of *usya* lands also varied from area to area, sometimes representing 10 percent of the total acreage, but often much more. Lands were usually divided into *ushuriyya*, which paid a 10 percent tax (*ushr*), and *kharajiyya*, which paid the higher tax. Frequently lands were turned into *usya* lands illegally, then into *waqf* or *rizqa* (a *waqf* of agricultural land) lands, equally illegally. By the end of the century one-sixth of the total arable land, 600,000 *faddans*, was *rizqa*, which paid little or no tax.

The peasants of the delta had the traditional right known as *athariyya*, the right to till the same land year after year (for in the delta the acreage of tilled land did not change with differences in the Nile flood) and to pass on that right to their heirs, to sell it, to mortgage it, or to include it in a *waqf*. The peasants of upper Egypt, however, had to wait each year to see the height of the Nile flood, when village lands would be measured and distributed among the villagers. In a bad year (that is, a low flood) some peasants were left landless. In too high a flood the villages might by flooded out. It was a constant cycle of feast or famine, but one good year did not balance a bad year.

By the end of the century those who had the authority to distribute such lands were the village heads, the *umdas* and shaikhs who dominated the village. They could thus distribute lands to their supporters. Should anyone entitled to till land die without any male heirs, the *umdas* could give the land to one of their relatives or keep it themselves. In some cases women sued to recover the right to till the land themselves when a father died leaving no male heirs. The eldest son inherited the plot from his father. Should the plot not be large enough to support other sons they became landless peasants, hiring themselves out to others who needed workers, or tried to find a wife whose father had no sons but had land, often a relative. The *fallah* had rights to the *usufruct* or use (*hiyaza*) of the land, including mortgage (*gharuqa*) or alienation to someone else, with the *multazim*'s approval.

As we have seen in Chapter 3, the tax-farmer came to use land as a commodity, an investment to be bought and sold. The introduction of cash crops for the export market made land more attractive as an investment by the middle of the century. Crops such as rice and sugarcane were the most lucrative, but they demanded a capital outlay; tax-farmers who had cash and rich farmers were the only ones who could afford to invest in such crops. Sugarcane, for example, needed two years to reach maturity. Abd al-Rahman Katkhoda al-Qazdaghli had three rice-growing villages in the region of Damietta. Thus when cash crops became a lucrative proposition those with ready cash, such as merchants and women as well as ulama, were the ones who bought up the tax-farms. However, in Damietta the *fallahin* cooperated with the merchants, who loaned them the money to grow rice. Muhammad Dada al-Sharaibi left tax-farms which yielded 1 million *paras* in profit. We have seen how Salun invested heavily in land, as did Nafisa Hanim al-Muradiyya and others.

The middle group of *fallahin* rose from among the *shaikhs al-balad* or *umdas* or bedouin tribal shaikhs. Some tribal shaikhs could easily rank among the elites because of their wealth, but they had no administrative positions, although the population looked upon them as notables. Among the bedouin tribal chiefs were powerful lords such as Shaikh Hummam of the Hawwara, reputedly the richest man in Egypt, the "prince" of upper Egypt until Ali Bey al-Kabir destroyed him; the Abazas, who headed the Aid clan; and the Lamlums, the Shawarbis, and others who were much less powerful.

The bedouin generally terrorized and exploited the peasants, but the two groups lived off each other. The bedouin forced the *fallahin* to pay them protection money and carted off their cattle and burned their crops if they refused. The bedouin also herded livestock. *Fallahin* rarely intermarried with bedouin, a practice that seems to have lasted to the present, yet the two groups had a symbiotic relationship.

The comfortably affluent *fallahin* were created out of a custom that allowed land, free of taxation, to be granted to village shaikhs in return for their good will; this was known as *masmuh al-mashayikh* or as *masmuh al-urban* when granted to the bedouin. A further category, *masmuh al-masatib*, was granted to village shaikhs to defray hospitality to wayfarers and government officials. It was customary for wayfarers to be given hospitality for three days at any village. Government officials were also granted hospitality. It was a different matter when the tax-farmers came round, as we shall see below.

Jabarti wrote that even the poorest villagers in the provinces would slaughter an animal for the dinner of any stranger or guest who arrived. This custom involved those other than the shaikhs and tribal leaders, who had guest houses (*madayif*), for guests, travelers, and the military.[50]

The *shaikh al-balad* or *umda* therefore had land on which he paid no taxes and also played a role as an intermediary between the village and the tax-farmer. Often the tax-farmer did not come to collect the taxes in person, but simply delegated the *umda* or sent an agent who arrived with a vast group of people (accountants, guards, etc.) who descended on the village, expecting hospitality for as long as they remained to collect the taxes. The taxes were assigned to the entire village (*kilala*), and the *umda* performed the same function as the guild shaikh, in that he assigned the percentage to be paid by every *fallah*. Should the village not make up the total sum, those who had money were forced to make up the deficit, for the entire village was responsible. The *umda* then would lend the villagers money.

Thus, while the *umda* looked after the rights of the villagers, he also exploited them as a moneylender. Because he had the power to assign land to the *fallahin*, he was clearly the most powerful man in the village. If any lands were unoccupied or their owners had died out, the *umda* could take over the lands or assign them to other *fallahin* for a fee. Umdas also controlled *awqaf* whose owners had died out and managed to accumulate wealth by these means. In that sense they represented the rural counterparts of the more affluent artisans. The rest of the *fallahin* represented the equivalent of the less affluent artisans, the small holders, while the landless *fallahin* were the rural equivalent of the urban poor.

Taxes and the tax collectors were the bane of the *fallahin*, along with the vagaries of the Nile and of nature in general. Famines and occasional epidemics wiped out entire villages (as did the malaria epidemic in the twentieth century during World War II). Often in crises the *fallahin* moved to the cities in the mistaken belief that they were running away from the plague or could find food in the towns.

Taxes were registered and officially recognized; but once an illegal tax was paid and registered, it too became recognized as an official tax. In that fashion some twenty-four different taxes were illegally forced on the fallahin. The legal tax was the *mal al-hurr*, which was paid to the *multazim* or his agents. This included the *miri* or land tax and two other legal taxes; whatever was left over was the tax-farmer's profit (*faiz*), so the more the tax-farmer could extort, the more his or her profit. The term *faiz* was also used to describe usury, one of the greatest sins in Islam. Next the *fallah* paid the "external tax," followed by the "added" tax, the impost, paid to the provincial governor, and hospitality dues to feed the tax-farmer and his or her horde plus the soldiers who accompanied them and the bedouin who threatened the security of the village.

Abuses could reach ridiculous levels. In the village of Zankalun, 1,225 *faddans* of an area of 5,314 *faddans* were *usya* and thus tax exempted. The more normal proportion would have been about 10 percent, not 23 percent as in that case. Zankalun paid 250,817 piastres as *faiz* (21.4 percent), only 169,231 piastres as *miri* (14.4 percent), and the outrageous sum of 751,200 piastres (64.1 percent) as an extra tax. Each tax-imposed *faddan* thus paid 286.5 piastres. Other areas usually paid half that sum or less.[51]

Taxes were collected in cash and in kind, especially in wheat and in barley, necessary for the mamluk cavalry. Daily rations in the regiments were 1 *ardab* (5.44 imperial bushels) of wheat and 1 of barley per man. This was supposed to feed one man and his horse for a day. It may have been enough for a gluttonous horse, but no man could eat that much. This was another way for mamluks to control and corner the grain market in addition to their ownership of most of the arable land.

Tax collecting time struck terror into the heart of the entire village. One unknown village bard, who may have been an alim, wrote a long poem describing those feelings. Professor Gabriel Baer interpreted the poem as being a diatribe by an urban dweller against the nasty habits of the rural people. Professor Abd al-Rahim correctly interpreted it as a sympathetic poem which depicted the harshness of life for the *fallah* and the exploitative nature of his relationship with the administration, as in the lines

My temples have whitened since nazlat al-kashif
And my heart has become all fear and trembling
The day when the *diwan* came, my bones loosened
And I doubt my own soul from fear.[52]

If the *fallah* had no money to pay the taxes that were demanded of him he was forced to sell any cattle he had, any jewelry his wife had (a form of capital popular among women of any stratum), and whatever else he could or to borrow money, frequently at usurious rates—for though usury is forbidden in Islam it was nonetheless practiced.

Frequently entire villages beat or killed the tax collectors or burned their crops and deserted their village so the tax collector could find nothing to collect and no one from whom to collect anything. Generally the *fallahin* were weighed down by burdens of tax arrears or by debts and usurious interest on debts, a situation which continued until the middle of the twentieth century. A cruel kind of relief came when plague or famine killed a number of the population and the remainder benefited by having more land to cultivate or when the death of the usurious moneylender eased the pressure of debt.

The *fallah* worked about 150 days in the year, since the rest of the time the land either lacked water or lay under water. Some areas close to the river were able to plant a summer lucrative crop, frequently cotton, watered by artificial devices such as the water wheel (*saqiya*) or the Archimedean screw (*shaduf*). The *fallah* decided when to work, how many hours to expend on his plot, and what crops to plant. Even among the small landholders cash crops were becoming widespread, especially those which did not need much capital, such as indigo.

The rest of the year the *fallah* and his wife labored at cottage industries. The peasant woman worked with her husband on the land and also raised fowls, which produced eggs for the market, and livestock for milk, butter (*ghee, samn*), or cheese. These she sold or bartered for other necessities in the weekly markets that were held in her own village or in villages that were within walking distances. For many, the walk was several hours back and forth. The *fallaha* also brought water from the river, which might be some distance from the village, in the morning and evening (unless the village was lucky enough to have a well or be on the river) and gathered cattle dung or stalks of various plants (such as cotton, wheat, or sugarcane) for firewood. Furthermore, she spun raw wool, cotton, and flax into thread and then wove the thread into textiles.

When Herodotus visited Egypt he described it as an odd country where the men sat indoors and wove and the women sat outdoors and talked. Times had changed by the eighteenth and nineteenth centuries, for women had little time to sit and talk. They worked constantly, even when their husbands did not, raising, feeding, and nurturing an extended family that could include three or more generations: the father, who worked the land, the sons who helped him on the land, and the grandchildren, who looked after the cattle, took them to graze, helped harvest, and took the midday meal to the fields. There might even be a grandparent still living who needed to be looked after. Idleness was not seen or encouraged in the rural areas.

Marriage was almost always between people from the same village, although *umdas* and *shaikhs al-balad* often married women of similar backgrounds from neighboring villages. The favored alliance was with the father's brother's son, to keep land and other property within the family. As Ken Cuno has shown,[53] wealthy peasants married other wealthy peasants, while middle-level peasants married within their own economic group, leaving the landless to marry daughters of other landless peasants. Occasionally a landless *fallah* married the daughter of a landed *fallah* if the father had no sons.

While women were allegedly denied access to miri land, they did in fact buy land. By then land was used as a commodity not only by the *multazims* but by the peasantry, who could buy and sell their right to *athariyya* land and could mortgage their land. The new tenant would then have the usufruct of the land for as long as the mortgage (*gharuqa*) lasted and could exchange land even when the land was theoretically not owned, because tenancy carried usufructory rights.

As previously noted, the concept of property was different in Muslim law than in the West. According to Muslim law there were gradations of ownership from possession or substance (which may or may not imply actual control, as in land which was crown domain) to properties of usufruct that could be sold or leased. Usufructory rights were possessed by peasants. The elites alone possessed the right to farm the taxes on the usufruct. Thus the same piece of land had three "proprietors" or people with different rights: the sultan, the tax-farmer, and the peasant.

Women did buy and sell land when they had the means to do so. But in a society where control of land in vast quantities meant political power and in smaller quantities meant subsistence, if not a degree of affluence, women among the poorer classes were often discriminated against when it came to inheriting land. The peasant in the delta inherited the *athariyya* right to till the soil and an obligation to pay the taxes. The *athariyya* was more frequently inherited by the eldest son than by a daughter, although there were exceptions to that rule. Women and men bought and sold land under Islamic law and Ottoman Egyptian custom for nearly a century before land became legislated into Western-style private property with the land law of 1858.

Upon marriage women received a dowry (*mahr*). In many cases the father used the money to outfit the bride and would be expected to add an equivalent sum of his own. Thus the bride would start married life as a property owner, whether the property included expensive silver anklets or merely a storage chest and a mattress. Such property was, in a sense, compensation for not inheriting her share of land if the family had any land. If the woman was divorced her back dowry (*muakhar*) had to be paid; if she died her back dowry entered her estate and was paid to her heirs. In several of the inheritances the loans to husbands by their wives were legally registered, so that the debt could be acknowledged and repaid in case of death or divorce. As previously noted, women occasionally sued their husbands in order to collect money owed them.[54] In one case the husband acknowledged the debt and promised to pay it back in monthly installments so long as the wife never laid any claim to any other part of his property.

Women inherited movable property, including agricultural tools, cattle, and buildings. Since the family was the basic unit of production every member was valuable. Women worked in the fields, produced for the market, bore children, nurtured and fed the family, and were recognized as property owners and were therefore an intrinsic and irreplaceable element in the productive unit. Yet while the male recognized her services to the household in most cases he was the one who controlled access to land and also the one who plowed the land, thereby acquiring the greatest power within the household, according to Goody. This could well be the father or grandfather rather than the son, who then was temporarily landless and worked for his father until he inherited that right himself. Problems arose when there was more than one son to inherit the land.

Whatever earnings the woman made generally went into a family pool, unless the woman had enough clout to keep her earnings for herself and her immediate family because she belonged to a richer family than her husband's and brought a sizable amount of property to the marriage or simply because she was assertive.

Within the urban or rural poor there may not have been a separation of property between men and women. Whatever both individuals earned was barely enough to keep body and soul together. Women could be threatened with divorce, an inducement to turn over their income to their husbands. Thus the most exploited women were the landless, wage-earning women, who had little enough leverage to use within the household. Their only bargaining powers were vested in their children or in their husbands' affections. Manipulation was again the only possible weapon. Just as the fallah used passive resistance to outwit the tax-farmer, the woman used passive resistance to outwit the man.

The town and the country, which lived off each other, were each stratified into a hierarchy. There was vertical mobility between the two spheres, for sons of *fallahin* became ulama and thus rose in the social scale or joined the town guilds of water carriers or of donkey boys. A relative who was an artisan and had no sons might adopt a *fallah* relative and teach him the trade and then marry him to his daughter. The village also had its artisans, for someone had to make and repair the machinery of the *shaduf* or the *saqiya*. As Cuno has pointed out, the village was not as cut off from the town as some scholars believed, for raw materials such as iron and wood came from the town, and the produce of the villagers was sold to the townspeople.[55]

Distance was the inhibiting factor that prevented the peasants from coming together to form guilds or other units for self-protection. Yet in rare cases peasants joined with others from neighboring villages to oppose the administration or to follow a leader, more often than not a religious figure, a Sufi mystic, who claimed to have special powers and who led the village in revolt.[56]

130

The peasants, much like the artisans in the towns, were not an inert mass that simply suffered persecution and exploitation. They reacted in a different fashion than the artisans. When aroused the artisans would drop their tools, close their shops, and march with their complaints to al-Azhar, where they hoped an *alim* would defend their cause and support their grievance, which often happened.[57] The peasants, as we have seen, manifested animosity by burning crops, purloining livestock, or fleeing to the hills or to the desert surrounding the village, so the tax collector could not find them. They could also move to another village which needed laborers. Such a practice was forcibly prevented in the nineteenth century, when irrigation projects had created more cultivable land and there was a shortage of peasants.

The strategies for resistance of the peasants were far different from those of the artisans and generally much more drastic. Passive resistance was followed by active resistance only when the level of exploitation exceeded bearable limits. The relationship between rulers and ruled, therefore, whether in the town or in the country, was a constantly shifting one in which the rulers sought to gauge the acceptable limits of extortion and the peasants sought the limits of resistance that would not lead to disaster. A continuing search for leadership in such circumstances resulted in leaders who were able to placate the populace and negotiate with the rulers or who preached resistance, as did Shaikh Sulaiman al-Jawsaki, head of the corporation (*taifa*) of the blind, who was executed by the French for leading an uprising against the French armies in Cairo.[58]

In summary, the rural milieu was as stratified as the urban milieu. In both women worked side by side with the men, but had the further burden of procreation as well as feeding and nurturing the members of the extended family. Although *fallah* women and men engaged in cottage industries, urban women usually did not, for work in the city was year-round while work in the countryside was largely seasonal. Thus while rural women could set a bit of income aside from their own activities (raising poultry, selling eggs, making and selling cheese and butter, even raising livestock), urban women probably did not have the same opportunities to produce surplus income apart from their husbands. This, of course, did not apply to women who were engaged in some activity of their own, such as the *ballanas*.

Whether rural or urban, the poorer classes and even the middle classes were afraid to face the administration directly because they were uneducated. Intermediaries acted as buffers between the rulers and the ruled; hence the importance of guild heads, shaikhs of *harat,* shaikhs of villages, tribal shaikhs, or potential intermediaries such as the ulama or the heads of mystic orders. Even on the personal level, quarrels between individuals, whether in town or country, were usually settled through intermediaries rather than by litigation, which was costly and long-winded.

When the intermediaries or buffers were removed during the administrative system instituted by Muhammad Ali in the nineteenth century, the population adapted an old institution now called by a new name: the *wasta* or intermediary, who would seek to placate or negotiate for the weak with the strong. The populace could not conceive of facing a bureaucrat on their own. They had been inured from the time of the Ottoman conquest to dealing with intermediaries rather than confronting the administration directly; authority was aloof and frightening. *Fallahin* saw the tax collectors going to the village with soldiers wielding whips to extract funds from the villagers. The urban people had always appealed to the ulama, who were their spokesmen, rather than face alien rulers, whether Ottoman or mamluk. The only administrative agencies the population was willing to deal with directly were the *sharia* courts, which were headed by ulama, in whom the population trusted. Women relied on the *sharia* courts to see that justice was done and believed that they would vindicate them and uphold their rights—an added proof of the influence the ulama had in society.

The basis for the fear of any confrontation with authorities was the average individual's ignorance of administrative procedures, which was a result of the arbitrary nature of the administration and of the fact that it was controlled by aliens, whether mamluks and their Syrian clients or, in 1798, the French. The relationship of absolute authority on the one hand and lack of power on the other undermined all administration dealings with the population and led to the creation of the institution of the intermediary.

The gulf between the rulers and the ruled as a consequence of the unequal power relationship or the presence of an alien ruling elite was perpetuated throughout the nineteenth and even the twentieth century and accounted for the constant state of alienation of the population (the *shaab* or *raaya* as the Ottomans referred to them) from the government (*hukuma*). It also accounted for the population's apparent disinterest in government, which is apparent in the low turnout of voters at the polls today. The rulers have done little to remove this centuries-old distrust.

6

THE NINETEENTH CENTURY
The Advent of Centralization

We have seen that in the eighteenth century women of all social groups (alien elites, indigenous elites, artisans and *ayan*, urban and rural lower classes) had access to all forms of property. Neither gender nor the seclusion of the elites prevented women from participating in the economic life of the country. Such access implied a role in public life in terms of participation in the marketplace as buyers, sellers, and investors. Given the economic power of the mamluk women it stands to reason that they also had access to centers of power either through influencing elite men or through contact with the ulama and the *tujjar*.

In her important work *Women in Nineteenth-Century Egypt*, Judith Tucker claims that the status of nonelite women declined in the nineteenth century. She attributes that decline to economic changes in which the state had little input or responsibility. "It was the process of integration of Egypt into a European economic system that weakened some guilds, especially those connected with textiles, and strained family and quarter organization by increasing landlessness and urbanization."[1]

Haim Gerber's valuable study *The Social Origins of the Modern Middle East* clearly shows that such assumptions are overstated.[2] Sherry Vatter's study of Damascene guilds corroborates Gerber by pointing out the strategies that enabled locals to survive in the face of European onslaught of goods.[3]

Tucker's statement that guilds, especially the textile guilds, were weakened in the latter half of the eighteenth century is correct. But this was not so much due to Egypt's entering the European economic system, as she claims, as it was the outcome of strategies of exploitation on the part of the ruling elite, with some European input. Mamluk government policies first undermined the situation of the weavers. By raising the price of raw material, the mamluks left the weavers little margin of profit, forcing many of them out of their trade and into unemployment. The high taxes imposed on the raw material exported to Europe filled the coffers of the mamluk beys and the Syrian merchants who ran the customs, who had invented that new form of taxation. Without the greed and connivance of the ruling elite such a change would not have been possible. Without the "pull" of the European market (the change in export policy), however, the "push" toward Europe would not have taken place.

When Muhammad Ali came to power in 1805 he further undermined the guild system for textiles by setting up state factories in 1820s and forbidding anyone to weave cloth outside these factories. Yet he was able to use the workers who had formerly been independent weavers as his industrial laborers in these same factories. In some cases women workers were employed in factories. Tucker is only partially correct in stating that weavers after Muhammad Ali "never regained their former levels of organizational strength...[women's] major productive link with the local market was greatly weakened."[4] The first part of this statement is not quite true: although the weavers' guild may have been weakened, E. R. J. Owen has shown that there were 28,000 textile weavers in 1870 (all male members of the guild),[5] a lot more than in the weavers' heyday in the eighteenth century. Guilds continued to survive and to play a role in Egyptian society until the end of the century, as Juan Cole's work on the Urabi revolution clearly demonstrates.[6]

The second part of Tucker's statement is true. Women did lose their links with the local markets, in part because of the growing ties with European trade, but more because of the new government's centralizing policies. Women lost out on their investments in looms and weaving areas because the government made it illegal to carry out such activities. Furthermore, many of the women who had made a living weaving lost their livelihood unless they accepted work in the new factories, side by side with men. Few women were willing to do that unless they were single parents and had no other means of support.

Tucker's statement that Egypt's integration into the European economic system strained family and quarter organization by increasing landlessness and urbanization is not correct. More land became available because of Muhammad Ali's irrigation; peasants therefore were not landless, although the increase in population as the century progressed resulted in landless peasants. What did change is that the peasants no longer possessed rights to work the land, as they had in the eighteenth century, but were hired as laborers to work the land. This may be what Tucker means by referring to them as landless. Urbanization undoubtedly increased under Muhammad Ali, but that did not necessarily militate against working women's earning a living since they were usually involved in trades that seldom conflicted with those involving males. It all depended on the sort of work women did, as we shall see below. The women who lost out were those who invested in the same kinds of money-making activities as men. The process of centralization and the new administration's largely successful efforts to control the state economy played the leading role in setting forth policies that led to the declining status of women, not the marginal role which Tucker attributes to the state.

By changing existing economic relationships Muhammad Ali's administration changed social relationships as well. First, the state changed land tenure laws. Second, the direction of commerce changed, gearing it toward Europe rather than the Ottoman Empire; in due course trade became totally integrated into the European world system, which contributed to further changes in economic and social life as well as patterns of consumption. Third, the state introduced institutions which militated against the participation of women in the economic life of the country.

The advent of Muhammad Ali to power signaled the introduction of a state system which was centralized and authoritarian. The ruler confiscated all tax-farms, claiming he would compensate the tax-farmers, which he did for a few years and then stopped. He also confiscated *waqf* lands unless the heirs could show property deeds, which many could not. A new cadastral survey was undertaken, the size of the *faddan* diminished, and land was redistributed according to the ruler's wishes in rewarding loyalty and service to himself and to the new state. Personal networks and political loyalties, which in the past were based on a number of competing households, were eliminated in favor of a different system of class rule centered on one household, that of the ruler. Loyalty went to the head of state, the originator of all benefits, *waliyy al-niam* as he was known in Arabic. Benefits took the form of land grants as protoprivate then private property, thereby hastening the proletarianization of the peasants of both sexes, but especially the men, who became wage earners rather than having legal rights to till a certain area of land. However, since there was much land available and fewer *fallahin*, landlessness or lack of land even for wage laborers was to become an issue much later in the century, and indeed in the twentieth century.

From 1811, when tax-farms were canceled, to the end of his reign, Muhammad Ali's government confiscated the old landholdings and gave land as private property to high officials and to the ruler's family and retainers. The new landowning groups were foreigners, Ottomans from various parts of the empire (Bosnians, Laz, Kurds, Armenians, Georgians, Greeks, Circassians) brought in with the new regime, former mamluks who had been induced to join the new administration, or native Egyptians who had become new bureaucrats, mostly in the lower ranks. Female members of the royal household (wives, concubines, and daughters) were also given grants of land, as were a few wives of select high government officials such as Nubar Pasha's wife.[7]

The ruling family ended by owning 663,048 *faddans* during Muhammad Ali's lifetime. That was to expand with successive regimes.[8] Women did not benefit from that land bonanza, unless they were members of the ruling elite's family or his closest retainers. In fact they lost out when their tax-farms were confiscated. Very few of them received any of the new lands, although later they did share in the land as part of inheritances.

For a while land stopped being a commodity one could buy and sell. In 1826 untilled land (*ibadiyya*) was offered tax-free or free of taxation for a number of years until it was cultivated. Many bedouin chiefs took advantage of that offer, as did some peasants. By 1837 usufruct of such lands became inheritable, and a few years later so did the land itself. These *bur* (untilled) and *ibadiyya* lands generally benefited the male elites, but they also contributed toward enlarging the native landowning class, for *umads* and *shaikhs al-balad* took advantage of these offers.

In 1836, when the ruler was again short of funds, he resorted to a new form of land tenure known as the *uhda* that resembled the old tax-farm system. Such lands were offered to anyone who undertook to pay their tax arrears and guarantee future taxes.[9] In return the new landowner was to leave the *fallahin* in possession of their right to cultivate the soil. The profit of the *mutaahid* (possessor of an *uhda*) was derived from cropping former fallow lands now brought under cultivation. Once this was done the landowner was supposed to turn the land over to the peasants. Whether the landowners ever did do so is moot. Many of these landowners were eventually dispossessed during the reign of Abbas (1265–1271/1848–1854) for failing to pay the taxes they owed.[10] The increase in land being brought under cultivation meant a greater need for peasants to work the land than heretofore. Each peasant was offered the opportunity to be employed, but the land was now owned and managed in different fashion. Whereas landlessness in the eighteenth century meant that peasants had no land to till, in the nineteenth century it meant that they had no prescriptive right to work the land, but were employed as laborers on it. All these changes in land tenure anticipated the land law of 1858. While land had become de facto private property under Muhammad Ali, this law made it de jure.

In an important dissertation on "Land Tenure in Rural Egypt: 1854–1863,"[11] Maha Ghalwash shows that the land law specified that land, unless it was owned by the elites, should be owned by those who needed it as a means of livelihood. The law specified that land held by peasants should be divided according to the *sharia* among the heirs, but only if they were capable of servicing the land, which implied that women could not inherit land unless they had males who could till the soil. If there were no males available then the women had to show proof that they needed the land as their sole means of support and not by right of inheritance. In the eighteenth century women had established inheritance rights to the land. The *sharia* courts abounded in such requests from women, who, contrary to Tucker's allegations, frequently won their cases and were granted inheritance rights to the land.[12]

The restriction of that right under Muhammad Ali was later legislated in the land law in 1858. From that period onward, as Ghalwash shows, when women inherited land they frequently registered it in their husband's or son's name, a change from the practice in the previous century, when women had been careful to register land in their own names, separate from their husbands' properties.[13] That tendency became exacerbated toward the end of the century.

The new *latifundia* that replaced the tax-farms may have changed hands, but the trend toward the accumulation of large tracts as opposed to smaller or medium-sized holdings continued until the middle of the twentieth century. The large majority of these landowners were men, with an exiguous proportion being elite women or women of the middle economic echelon who had inherited land. Jeffrey Collins notes that in 1880 women small property holders amounted to 9 percent, women holding medium-sized lands amounted to 15 percent, and women holding large properties amounted to 10 percent.[14] While such percentages do not seem negligible if we assume that investment in land was only one option, they become striking when investment in land became the only option toward the end of the century, as we shall see.

The change in land tenure also included the annulment of hereditary peasant rights to till the same piece of land and not to be ousted from the land unless they had failed to pay the taxes for three consecutive years. The peasants were now turned into wage laborers working on lands owned, not by the sultan, but by private landowners. It is true that land was plentiful and owners wanted peasant laborers, so they may have treated them better than under the old regime as the British consul-general, Henry Salt, claimed.[15]

The advent of wage labor introduced new gender relationships as well. Labor was now mobilized around the nuclear family, where the man became the breadwinner, a wage laborer; the work of a woman peasant tended to be unrewarded since what she produced was supposedly for subsistence. Women became regarded as mere dependents and as a reserve labor force to be used when men were needed in the army or in factories. In point of fact this was a means of paying women less than a male wage laborer since the womenfolk were actually working alongside the men, as hard and as long, but for free. During harvest time women and children helped out in the fields; if and when they were paid by the landowner, it was a pittance compared to a man's wages. Where a man might receive a wage of six to eight piastres, women were paid two to four piastres.[16] Women continued to raise poultry and livestock and make cheese and ghee. They attended the weekly markets, which were often some distance away. Though such labor may have supplemented the family income substantially, men's contribution to the family welfare was assumed to be the more important. Over time the notion that man was the primary if not sole breadwinner became more firmly established, and woman's functions were pushed to the periphery. She and her children were perceived as dependents on the father's earnings and not as an intrinsic part of the family productive unit. The family therefore echoed the central formation of the state.

As the state developed a hierarchy with a pyramidal structure headed by the ruler, reigning over a civil bureaucracy subservient to his wishes and from whom all advantages flowed, so the family became a hierarchy, with the male ruling at the top. Industrialization and the new market economy sustained the state but undermined the concept of the family as a productive unit, replacing it with the individual, even though the entire family worked on the land in farming and at times was hired to work in industry, as in the arsenal.

Not only did the state become the model for male domination of the family, but male authority was reinforced legally through the appearance of the Mecelle (the legal code issued by the Ottoman government), which codified the *sharia* and stressed the secondary role of women, and ideologically through newly imported European ideas.

The conscription of men for the army, for public works projects, and as laborers on the land of the powerful increased women's domestic workload. They frequently followed the men to feed and look after them while they worked on corvée public works, even having to earn enough to support the family while the men worked on corvée and at the same time nurturing their children. If they stayed behind in the village they were forced to take on the men's labor. The new *izba* (estate/ *latifundia*) system added to the male's importance, for now every wage earner lived in a house provided by the landowner on his *izba*; should the *fallah* ever lose his job he would also lose his home.

Other events, including a rising degree of exploitation, changed the peasant's lifestyle. In the past the peasant had worked 150 days a year and planted what he wanted, mostly crops that he could eat; now he worked 100 days more and the government, later the landowner, told him what to plant, when to plant it, and how to plant it.[17] During the period of subsistence agriculture the peasant had grown food crops to feed his family and his animals, but in a cash crop economy he was forced to grow crops for the market—over which he had no control—which regulated the prices at which products were bought and sold. Whatever cottage industries the fallah or his family had carried out were prohibited by the state.[18] Whether the extra wages he received for working longer days compensated for that loss or not remains unknown.

When Egypt was bankrupted and the British occupation took place in 1882, much of the land that the Khedive Ismail owned was sold off as Daira Saniyya (*khedival*) land and sale of domains land. Out of 730 sales of Daira Saniyya lands with a total acreage of 162,263 *faddans*, only one buyer was a Christian woman: Katrina Fahmi Yusif bought 120 *faddans* in al-Rawda.[19] In the registers bearing the names of *dhawat* (gentry) owning *ushuriyya* land (which paid the tithe), which included the large landowners of the country, no independent women owners are cited. Landowners are generally referred to as "so and so and his wife."[20] Women were reduced from being 15 percent of the tax-farmers to becoming 10 percent of the large landowners. Although land tenure was only one venue of investment for women in the eighteenth century, by the nineteenth century all indigenous wealth came from land only, so women lost out on income-producing venues even more than the percentages would lead one to assume.

The same handicaps in owning land operated among the male local elites, especially the high ulama. The high ulama had owed their economic well-being to the supervision of charitable endowments and to rewards reaped from their links to the mamluks and the regiments which paid them salaries. By 1811 Muhammad Ali had disbanded the regiments, canceled regimental salaries except for the soldiers, and confiscated charitable endowments, which were now directed by the state. This impoverished the religious schools (*kuttab*), which were financed by *awqaf*, as indeed were the salaries of the ulama teaching in them.

Furthermore, having been brought to power by the ulama and the merchants, Muhammad Ali sought to diminish the ulama's power over the masses by taking away their benefits derived from other sources, making them rely on the state for their incomes. From then on the position of the ulama, in effective politico-legal terms, began to decline.[21] Mohammad Ali did, however, recompense those among the ulama who supported him with small grants of land.

Functions previously carried out by the ulama were taken over by state bureaucrats. This trend continued after Muhammad Ali. In 1859 litigation over lands which paid the government tax, for example, was removed from the jurisdiction of the muftis and made the concern of the adminis-tration.[22] By the end of the century the *sharia* courts were limited to litigation dealing with matters of personal status: marriage, divorce, and inheritances other than land. The influence of the ulama was further eroded by the introduction of secular education, which displaced the one remaining monopoly, other than religion, of the ulama.

By the twentieth century the ulama were relegated to purely religious matters. They were displaced as teachers of Arabic by graduates of Dar al-Ulum and by graduates of the secular schools. One should not minimize the part played by religion in any society, but once the ulama began to receive government salaries their ability to be neutral and to serve as arbiters of disputes was eroded. The continuing loss of power by the high ulama had a further consequence affecting women. Where in the past women had appealed to the ulama to protect them from abuse and to protect their rights, as we have seen in the previous chapters, the ulama no longer had the same clout with the administration. They could use appeals to the *sharia* and their personal influence to support the rights of women, but once they had become marginalized from government affairs they could no longer exert as much pressure.

The government under Muhammad Ali sought to dominate and eventually to monopolize all trade and commerce. Merchants were divided and had conflicting interests. One lot of mostly minority merchants traded with Europe and pushed for expanding that trade route. They exported raw materials and imported finished goods, which of course affected the artisans negatively. In consequence the artisans were ready to take arms against the system when they found leaders to encourage them to do so. Umar Makram armed and paid the artisans to rise against the French and later to rise against the Ottomans in support of Muhammad Ali. When Muhammad Ali came to power he hanged the heads of the guilds of butchers and of vegetable sellers, who had helped bring him to power, in order to end any potential resistance to himself and eventually exiled Umar Makram.

The second lot of merchants were those dealing with trade in the Red Sea, hitherto the most lucrative of trade routes. Dominated by wealthy merchants such as Mahruqi and Muwailhi, they encouraged Muhammad

Ali to invade Arabia, ostensibly to put down the Wahhabi revolt, but actually to renew trade with Mecca, which had come to a standstill because of insecure routes. Muhammad Ali at first sided with the Red Sea merchants, but later saw that he could make more money, which he sorely needed if only to pay his soldiers, by selling wheat and other food crops to the European market, especially the British fighting the peninsular wars.

Support for merchants involved in European trade, in an effort to make more money for the ruler and his projects, resulted in his monopoly on all agricultural produce. This had to be sold to the government, which then sold it to European merchants or back to the population at prices set by the government. Furthermore, in efforts to expand the European market Muhammad Ali invited European merchants to settle in Egypt, hoping to use their networks in Europe to expand his commercial holdings. In 1836 there were 3,000 European merchants, where thirty years earlier there had been only 2. By 1878 foreign merchants had reached 68,000, many of whom were given large grants of land by the rulers or bought estates. The land of the Daira Saniyya that had been left unsold, which amounted to 308,122 *faddans*, was sold by E. Baring, later Lord Cromer (British consul-general and uncrowned king), to French and British nationals, four of whom bought up the entirety of the remainder in 1898.[23]

Local merchants were thus cut out both in international trade and in buying up Daira Saniyya lands. They either joined the administration as bureaucrats or had to find another profession. Furthermore, the treaty of Balta Liman signed between England and the Ottoman Empire in 1839 specified that all imports were to pay a 5 percent ad valorem tax, while exports paid a 12 percent duty and goods in transit paid 3 percent.[24] Thus foreign merchants, who mostly imported commodities, were clearly favored over the local merchants who exported local goods.

In addition foreign merchants abused the prerogatives granted by the Capitulations. (In the sixteenth century these were rights to trade in the Ottoman Empire granted to European merchants, but as the Ottomans weakened militarily by the nineteenth century they became rights of extraterritoriality for Europeans—a means of evading local laws.) They refused to pay the local taxes, which were borne by their native counterparts. Thus, even after the state ceased to be the sole monopolist, native merchants found themselves in a much weaker position than the European merchants, who also had extensive networks in Europe whereas the locals had none. There was thus "a complete change of the commercial system where local merchants suffered oppressive taxes and duties but the foreigners were exempted."[25] The foreign merchants had links with local retailers through intermediaries, who were often minorities.[26] Foreign governments supported their merchants and pushed their claims whenever they could.

David Landes in *Bankers and Pashas* has shown how spurious many of these claims were and how helpless the Egyptian rulers were to dismiss them.[27] Perhaps the most outrageous claim was the one made by Ferdinand de Lesseps, who sued the Egyptian government when he ran out of funds to finish the Suez Canal. The issue went to arbitration, the arbiter being Napoleon III, whose wife, Eugénie, was the cousin of de Lesseps and who had been given, in secret, large chunks of shares in the canal as a bribe. Naturally he ruled in favor of de Lesseps and Egypt incurred a large debt, borrowed to pay the indemnity imposed on it.[28]

Women investors were the main ones to suffer from that situation. They no longer had the networks with the merchants and the marketplace in general that had allowed them to invest in commerce and that kept them informed as to the affairs of the marketplace. The state had displaced the merchants, and commerce became a monopoly at the hands of the ruler. The new merchants were Europeans who had no contact with local women. Local men who developed contacts with the Europeans may not have been part of the women's former networks or may have chosen to invest on their own account, so that even if they used the women's funds they were invested in the names of the males. Owen points out the domestic market became dominated by European manufactures from 1840, when foreign merchants even invaded the countryside.[29]

It is clear that both local men and women suffered from competition with European merchants, but men were able to rally and create new networks while women were not as successful. Their husbands were no longer absentees and were not afraid of confiscation, since all bounty came at the hand of the ruler who rewarded his military and bureaucracy. Ancillary businesses such as *wikalas* and storehouses also suffered, for now the government used its own storehouses and its own shops to sell commodities. Foreign merchants moved into the main bazaars and wikalas, displacing local men. A few women did continue to invest in "bourgeois trading circles" and joined commercial associations; in 1856 "women invested in sea trade of spices and the caravan slave trade."[30] As that trade diminished and fell into other hands and slavery was prohibited, women's participation became nullified.

During the eighteenth century there seems to have been a de facto *séparation de biens* within a marriage, with property belonging to the wife clearly demarcated as such, but after 1858 that separation was no longer clear and the woman's property was often merged with that of her male relatives. According to Islamic law the male is responsible for all the household expenditures, so women could use their funds to do whatever they pleased. But when a woman's income became merged with that of her husband or son it was invariably the male who controlled that income.

Crafts were still practiced by working-class women, but skilled trades were closed to them: "State training policies assigned skilled labor to men."[31] Women were not employed in factories or mills that used steam power. Women's role in the production of the urban economy "contracted . . . by the end of the nineteenth century, working women became concentrated in this world of casual services and informal networks."[32]

Why did women acquiesce to such a system—or, more importantly, did they have a choice? The answer to both these questions is that they had no choice. Women tax-farmers were the only ones to demonstrate against Muhammad Ali's attempts to take over their profit, but the tide was too strong for them, especially when the entire system changed.

Muhammad Ali's first problems were how to dominate and centralize authority and how to change those institutions which prevented him from doing so. By then the alien and native elites were sorely divided. The mamluk houses were busy fighting one another when they were not fighting the new ruler, so it was simple enough to destroy them or coopt them into the new administration. Any disturbances on the part of the ulama were smothered by confiscating their financial resources, and any disturbances in the rural areas were defused by setting up industries or later conscripting *fallahin* into the army.

Muhammad Ali and his successors had set out to modernize the country, a process accelerated by the British occupation. Modernization implied the incorporation of new institutions such as banks, the stock market, insurance companies, and joint stock companies. All of these were inventions from Europe, where the legal economic existence of a woman separate from her husband was not recognized—a woman's property was managed by her father, husband, or brother. Egyptian women were faced with the same obstacles; the new institutions did not recognize their legal right to invest in their own names, so they had to have a male relative as an agent, an intermediary. When her husband held the checking account, invested in the companies, and did all the buying and selling, the woman found herself totally out of the picture.

Women could still own houses and indeed continued to own real estate for investment throughout the century, but whatever shops they owned catered to the artisanal trade, which was sadly reduced even though it continued to survive. Such shops could only supply a modest income and therefore were of interest only to the middle to poor strata. Many artisans eventually found their markets diminished because European commodities were flooding the market and were being sold in new stores set up in new sections of the city. Hanna notes that in the eighteenth century, when Ottoman influence was at its weakest, certain Ottoman terms began to be used in houses (*oda* for *qaa, cesme* for *sabil* or drinking fountain, etc.).[33] Under Muhammad Ali and his successors, who tried to act as though they were Ottomans culturally when they were breaking away from the empire politically, that trend continued. A new trend of copying things European was added. Fashion, led by the court and its hangers-on, introduced European clothing, furniture, architecture, utensils, even musical instruments. All of these were imported and sold by European merchants and undermined the local market.

The women of the new elites were wives of bureaucrats, mostly Ottoman Egyptian or foreign born, coming from various parts of the Ottoman Empire or Europe, and were not allowed to have a free hand in the marketplace as mamluk and native women had. These women lived isolated and segregated. The new native bureaucrats who were to rise in the ranks through a process of Egyptianization of the bureaucracy throughout the century tried to imitate their elite superiors in their lifestyles and also segregated their women. In this they were followed by the new middle class. Thus women who had previously not been veiled and segregated now found themselves in harems, just like their social superiors. Women who formerly had been free to circulate in the marketplace were now unable to do so.

"Modernization," a term that implied a centralized state system, a new bureaucracy, new technology, new secular education, increasing urbanization, different customs imported in imitation of the Ottoman customs—for Muhammad Ali fancied himself an Ottoman gentleman, unlike his son Ibrahim, who felt himself to be Egyptian[34]—and more rigid mores, militated against the participation of women in the marketplace. Certainly in the case of education women were sent to the end of the line. Muhammad Ali opened a series of schools, all of which were meant to produce better officers and bureaucrats, not to educate in the wide sense. Though he himself forced his daughters to become as educated as his sons, he did not mean to educate the population and even less the female part of it. He did open a school for midwives in 1832, but nothing further was done until the 1870s. Whether the school for midwives employed as many midwives as existed outside the school is dubious. Whatever education for girls had existed in previous centuries continued during most of the nineteenth century.

Thus men began to acquire a new education, different from the religious instruction previously received by both sexes, but women did not. Under the mamluks both sexes were equally illiterate or received similar educations; neither sex had an edge over the other. With the new century and the new secular education the educational gap between men and women began to grow in terms of acquisition of knowledge, not just mere literacy, although even in literacy the gap became enormous. Thus in addition to preferential treatment in training and technology, men were given an educational edge.

Late in the century the first schools for girls opened, and literacy among women became an issue expressed in the new "feminist" literature adumbrated in *The Emancipation of Women* and *The New Woman*, two books written by a magistrate, Qasim Amin. Newspapers and magazines published for women and written by women appeared, addressing especially women's educational needs.[35]

Men could use the gap in education to limit women's involvement in the marketplace, for now women could be told that they could not understand enough to participate in the financial and economic markets or even to understand accounts. This gap was widest among the elite since both sexes of the lower classes remained illiterate. By the 1870s there was a movement toward opening schools for women, but a decade later the British occupation hindered the push toward the expansion of education for both sexes. Furthermore, since men lived longer now that elites were no longer involved in life and death struggles against each other, the generational gap between spouses began to grow larger since men had to establish themselves in the bureaucracy before marriage, giving men an edge over their younger and less-educated wives and strengthening patriarchy, already mirrored in the government and the ruler.

Through its monopoly of justice, political power, and labor obligations the state replaced whatever previous systems had existed by male bureaucrats and a strictly hierarchical system. The male bureaucrat who had spent his day being harassed in his job, if only by his superior, returned home demanding comfort and service from his wife and children, who catered to him in return for his financial support. Wage-earning women were expected to serve others in the family. (But this is nothing new in history.) The business world and the world of politics formed the outside sphere where the individual found himself engaged in stressful behavior which required that he develop traits of aggression, intelligence, and self-interest, while the home became the inner world where the wage earner relaxed, was served, and lorded it over the household. Meanwhile the urban homebody was expected to develop gentleness, self-abnegation, service to others, obedience, and the art of nurturing.[36] It would seem that slave/mamluk women had been freer in their households than free wives were in theirs.

Such a division in society had developed in the West a nineteenth-century ideal of the idle elite and bourgeois woman who did not work outside the house, who was "silly," "dependent," "decorative," and "sentimental." Women were transformed into children to be guided by their rational menfolk, for they could only be emotional and sentimental. Even the roles assigned to women—the realm of morality and child rearing—became trivialized.[37]

As for the working woman, she was exploited unmercifully, as was the working man, and was certainly not a model for anyone; in the past she had served a definite productive function, but now the state assigned her a secondary function working at jobs which none of the men wanted.

There are those who might argue that women in the Muslim world had already been trivialized by their seclusion over the ages. The *haramlik* and the *salamlik* did divide the world of the elite woman into an inside and an outside sphere. But so long as women were able to become involved in the marketplace they could not be as totally trivialized as they were in the nineteenth century. Muslim women possessed legal existence in the outside world as property owners, a right which European women forfeited when they were married and property passed into the legal keeping of their spouses. Yet in the nineteenth century Egyptian women became as trivialized as their sisters in Europe precisely because of changes in government, the creation of new institutions, and the development of a centralized state that controlled, dominated, and directed the means of production, thereby mobilizing the resources of the state.

Concrete changes in the form of government which resulted in centralization of all resources in the hands of the state (i.e., the ruler and his cohorts), changes in the means of production, and changes in technology caused changes in the position and role of some men and most women in society. Why did women not take advantage of the new technology being introduced? They were not permitted to do so by the state. When new technologies that demanded a period of apprenticeship or training were introduced, women were pushed to the bottom of the ladder and told they were incapable of learning such technology. Bridget Hill has shown that early in the eighteenth century English women worked as blacksmiths and bricklayers, but when the new technology came in women were barred from these very same professions.[38] E. M. Cheney and M. Schmink have found that Latin American women had limited access to modern technology, for as tools became more sophisticated women were "eased out of the most 'modern' sectors." Technological innovation "can change the sex label of a job." They conclude that "the more closely allied a society becomes to Western development models . . . the more we can expect women to be excluded from the tools of the production process," which leaves women with the unskilled, lower-paying jobs.[39]

That attitude was clear in early days of manufacture in Egypt. Prejudice against women on the part of the foreign experts who were imported to teach the Egyptians the new technology prohibited women from working in steam-powered textile mills under Muhammad Ali, for the experts claimed that women could not learn to use the new machines. Foreign not local prejudice militated against women's acquisition of a new technology.

Though poorer peasant women became more dependent on the male members of the family, most continued to do what they had always done, so rural women have never become as peripheralized as urban women. Furthermore, rural markets were eventually less controlled by the state than the urban ones; women could set the prices for their products or, better yet, could use a barter system that suited them.

The real changes came in the situation of women of the elite and the middle classes. Women of the elite no longer possessed tax-farms and most frequently turned over their land to males. The sole exceptions were women of the royal family, who were given large tracts of land by the royals. New institutions militated against women's participation in the market-place.

As for family and neighborhood organizations, one must differentiate between the urban and the rural family as well as between different social strata. The petit bourgeois urban family continued to function as it had always done; the neighborhoods and local communities (*hitta* and *hara*) continued to survive until the end of the nineteenth century and well into the twentieth century in the old quarters of Cairo. Naguib Mahfouz's novel *Awlad Haritna* perpetuates the idiom of the "children of the quarter" forming a unit of solidarity, as do his other novels (*Midaq Alley*, *Palace Walk*, etc.), which present examples of the continued existence of the local community and its networks. There were changes, especially in the new quarters built for the new elites. Muhammad Ali Street, for example, cut across a number of quarters, upsetting communal relations.

The major changes came with the building of new quarters—such as the area round the new Abdin Palace built by Khedive Ismail and the Mubtadayan, where the new elite built their mansions, or Abbasiyya, which became a new suburb of Cairo under Abbas—and the introduction of new housing styles. These palazzi, built in a European style adapted to local needs, were surrounded by large gardens, cutting them off from the street, and by high walls which kept the women in isolation. While elite women visited their friends and relations regularly, each woman holding a weekly "at home," they had no outlet or interest in their quarter as an institution.

These changes were a consequence not so much of Egypt's entering the world market, but of the new institutions set up by the state as part of state policies and the sycophantic relationship that existed between the ruler and his bureaucracy. Abbas, for instance, forced his generals to buy land and build houses in Abbasiyya. Others built houses round Ismail's new palace in Abdin and the Mubtadayan. Many of the new elites adopted the European outlook toward women, probably not because they thought that it was better or more "modern" but because it allowed them greater control over women's property. In the case of the richer *fallahin*, it allowed the males to prevent female family members from owning land. One means of so doing was to buy land in the names of sons, but do nothing for the daughters, who would then inherit, along with their brothers, only the parcels of land that were left in the common inheritance.

Women who reacted negatively to such discrimination were told that their husbands were responsible for their welfare and that their daughters should inherit property from their fathers not from their maternal grandfathers, even though that degree of inheritance was specified in the Quran. Not all males were so adamant in leaving their land to their male descendants, but women who inherited land generally left its management to the male members of their family, especially if property was left in common, undivided, and managed by male relatives, who may or may not have treated their female relatives fairly.

Urban women landowners, as absentee owners, were cheated by the peasantry and received very little income from the land—an added reason for the males to take over direction and management of rural property, rather than teaching those who were ignorant how to manage it.

Whereas in the past the tax-farmer had sent armed representatives to collect the dues, now they were being collected by the *umdas*, who more often than not were the ones cheating the landowners. The peasantry cheated any absentee landlord, male or female, but were more blatant with women, who could not represent themselves unless they had male relatives who would look after their interests and who knew something about cultivation. Frequently urban elites, usually nonnative Egyptians, knew

little about cultivation and depended on their overseers or their accountants, who ended up possessing more land than the original owners by
cheating the people who employed them. These elites often could not
speak Arabic and could not even communicate with their agents among the
peasantry.

We can thus see a clear social change: in the eighteenth century the
native elites were ulama and merchants; in the nineteenth century the
native elites were government employees or village shaikhs and *umdas*,
some of whom in time became large landowners. From the mid-nineteenth
century on those who controlled land became wealthy. In the eighteenth
century wealth could be derived from trade and commerce; in the
nineteenth century trade and commerce became monopolized by foreigners, and the wealth of the native population was predominantly derived
from land.

Urban wealth was acquired by owning buildings and shops, many of
which were owned by foreigners who traded in newly imported commodities. By the late nineteenth and early twentieth century major department
stores had been set up, all owned by Jewish foreign nationals: Ades
(English), Cicurel (French), Orosdi Bak (Austrian), Chemla (French),
Gattegno, (Italian), and others.

The marginalization of both men and women was a slow process. It
took three or four decades to accomplish and was accompanied by the
marginalization of other social groups, as we have seen. Occasionally an
anomaly such as a woman coffee house owner who was also the head of a
gang of *futuwwat* (toughs) is mentioned; but by and large, until well into
the twentieth century, when the nationalist movement allowed elite
women to come out of their harems and become involved in the socioeconomic life of the country, urban elite women owned houses and small
shops in the poorer quarters. As Charles Issawi and others have shown,
most of the businesses were owned by foreigners. A few members of the
native population did show entrepreneurial talents (for example, the
Banque Misr industries), but most of the population was limited in its
spirit of enterprise by foreign competitors.

The rest of the population had to wait for the Revolution of 1952,
which brought radical changes when it nationalized foreign banks and
insurance companies. Even more importantly, the new regime introduced

mass education, from which the women greatly benefited. Earlier regimes had made university education free, but the new regime allowed a greater influx into the universities, especially of older people, who were encouraged to acquire a school leaving certificate through adult education, qualifying them for entrance into the universities. Many women who had been married early in life took advantage of these new rules to become university graduates. Furthermore, the new regime opened certain faculties that in the past had been closed to women or had discriminated against women, such as the faculty of engineering.

There are those who would argue that women who are limited to the home are not being marginalized but glorified and respected. Gender relations are modified by economic realities and conditions. When the husband becomes the sole wage earner and the woman is simply "surplus" labor the woman becomes a "dependent." The man, who makes the money, is the linchpin of the household; the principle of "equal but different," the rallying cry of the Muslim activists, is voided. The more wealth a woman controls, the more weight within the family she acquires and, naturally, the less dependence. The contrary is also true. There are, of course, exceptions. The position of the mother is a powerful one vis-à-vis her male children, but it is less powerful in the face of a husband who can use divorce or the implied threat of divorce and separation from her children.

Throughout history both men and women have had to shift strategies in order to adapt to changing conditions. I have attemped to show how women tried to take advantage of social and economic conditions in the seventeenth and eighteenth centuries to participate in the economic life of the country. This allowed them a certain clout. Far from being a stagnant society, in Egypt the eighteenth century was a period of change and adaptation for women. Women found ways of maintaining and expanding their presence in the marketplace and of accumulating independent wealth.

In the nineteenth century state policies marginalized women. Activities of women of the urban elite and the bourgeoisie were limited to the home. Working-class women became dependent on the male wage earner. Rural peasant women found their economic and social relations modified by the new landholding laws and the change to market-oriented export crops. Secular education became the means of administrative and bureaucratic advancement and was denied to women.

As for the men, they too faced changes. The peasant was dispossessed and became a wage earner; the more affluent peasants became part of the new landowning class of *ayan*. The wage earner was exploited with longer working hours and divested of his surplus earnings through the abolition of cottage industries. Because he was paid a wage he assumed that he was the primary breadwinner in the family. As the population grew in numbers and land became scarce, male peasants resented women's control of any land and tried to cut women out of land ownership.

Large *latifundias* were created by state policies and often owned by absentee landlords. Many of these landlords, especially if foreigners, were soon displaced by their local agents, who cheated them out of their lands. Local merchants were displaced by European merchants and thus concentrated on internal trade or trade with the Sudan. Any surplus funds they had were also invested in land. The government bureaucrat replaced the former native elites as the source of authority and the focus of power.

In brief, the modern state system did not advance the position of women—it pushed them back into the home as secondary citizens. Today "modern" states encourage women to go out into the marketplace when they need more labor power then push women back into the home when jobs become scarce and women compete with men for them. Rosie the Riveter is one famous example in the West, but such examples are multiple in the Third World. One by-product of such attitudes is the rise of *intégriste* movements which encourage women to become dependents so as not to take scarce jobs away from men, almost trying to duplicate the condition of elite women in the nineteenth century. They tell women who need to work or who desire to work because highly trained that they can take jobs which serve only women, but not those which serve men, or they encourage them to apply for lower-paying jobs which men do not want. Women who are part of the paternalistic system accept such differentiation, especially when it is wrapped up in religious terminology.

The rare voices of ulama like the contemporary Shaikh al-Ghazali, who pointed out that there is no blemish (*awra*) in women and that they are entitled to seek work just as much as men, are refreshing in the contemporary world. The strength of these voices and others like them will depend on the politics and economic outcome of the next few decades.

APPENDIX A
Mamluk Elites

1. Arifa Khatun, daughter of Abdallah al-Baida, in 1184/1770, freedwoman of the deceased Sulaiman, Katkhoda Mustahfazan, and *nazira* of a *waqf* set up by her deceased husband, al-Haj Yusif al-Jabi of the *mustahfazan* al-Shaarawi, exchanged her interest of 12/24 *qirats* in a house (*hikr*) in a *waqf* of which she is the *nazira* in return for 350 *riyal pataques* from her husband, Mustafa Bakir al-Maltili (*azaban*). The document gives us the added information that the lady had two husbands, three if we asssume that Sulaiman Katkhoda had married her, from the *mustahfazan* regiment; the third a member of the *azaban* who later joined the *mustahfazan*. *Mahfadha 7, hujja* 302.

In 1186/1772 Arifa exchanged her right to 2/24 *qirats* of a house in a *waqf* over which she was *nazira*, belonging to her dead husband, in favor of her present husband, Mustafa Bakir Mustahfazan (note that he is now identified with the *mustahfazan* and not the *azaban* regiment), follower of Ibrahim Shurbaji, in return for the sum of 250 *riyals* (22,500 paras). *Mahfadha 7, hujja* 319.

2. Khadija Khatun, former slave of Amir Ahmad Bey al-Aasar, in 1185/1771 turned a house into a *waqf* of which she was the *nazira* during her lifetime. After her death, her husband, Ismail al-Barquqi, was to become the *nazir*. *Mahfadha 8, hujja* 383.

3. Arifa Khatun, daughter of Abdallah al-Baida, freedwoman of Amir Husain al-Kabir al-Qazdaghli, in 1186/1772 paid 1,500 gold dinars in exchange for a property owned in a *waqf* set up by Kanja Khatun Abdallah

155

through her agent, Muallim Yaqub the Christian, son of Muallim Yuhanna al-Saidi. *Mahfadha 7, hujja* 350, 352.

The same lady, who was married to Mahmud Katkhoda Husain al-Qazdaghli, clearly her former owner's *katkhoda*, in 1189/1775 ceded her right to a property that was a *waqf (hikr)* to Khadija Khatun, manumitted slave of Ahmad Bey al-Aasar and wife of Ismail, follower of Muhammad Effendi al-Barquqi, for the sum of 2,000 *riyals* (18,000 *paras*). (See no. 2 above.)

4. This deed announced the death of Aisha Khatun, bint Abdallah al-Baida, in 1186/1772 and revealed her heirs to be her husband, Ali Aga, and the two sons of the man who had manumitted her, Haj Ali al-Jazairli. *Mahfadha* 8, *hujja* 400.

5. In 1186/1772 Hanifa Khatun, daughter of Abdallah al-Baida, and her husband, Amir Khalil Abdallah Shawushan, acquired equal shares in a property belonging to the *waqf* of Amir Mustafa Abdallah Tufekjiyan in return for 2,135 *riyal pataques*. (Note this Hanifa may in fact be Arifa no. 3 through a scribal error in names.) *Mahfadha* 8, *hujja* 366.

6. Fatima Khatun, daughter of Abdallah al-Baida, who is identified ethnically as a Georgian, freedwoman of Shaikh Ibrahim, Katib Qalam al-Khorda, and wife of Amir Ali Odabasha Azaban, in 1187/1773 renounced her rights in a portion of 1.3/24 *qirats* in an *iltizam* in return for a *hulwan* (fee) of 630 *riyals*, paid to her by her husband and received by her follower Jawhar Aga Abdallah. *Mahfadha 7, hujja* 329.

7. Saliha Khatun, daughter of Abdallah al-Baida, freedwoman and wife of Uthman Shurbaji Mustahfazan, in 1187/1773 left an inheritance that listed the following items: a little over 1 *qirat* in a *makan* (property) and the same share in another four other *makans*, a *rab*, a weaving establishment, a large *makan* (*kabir*), two shops and a mill and their appurtenances, and a *hawsh*. Q.A. 190, folder 578, p. 472.

8. Khadija Khatun, daughter of Abdallah al-Baida, freedwoman of Ahmad Qarabas, in 1187/1773 set up a *waqf* of 41 *uthmanis* (gold coins

each worth 123 *paras*) a house, and five shops which are a *hikr* (that is, *waqf*), with their ground rent dedicated to the Haramain, plus ten shops and the buildings above them, the revenue to be spent on five Quran reciters to recite from the Quran for her soul and the souls of her children and her retainers and freed slaves and those of all dead Muslims. The reciters were to be paid 150 *nisf fidda* per month, the rest of the money to be expended on various charities. *Mahfadha* 7, *hujja* 328.

9. Fatima Khatun, daughter of Abdallah al-Baida, freedwoman of Ahmad Odabasha Mustahfazan Shahin, in 1187/1773, through her agents Murjan Aga and Bashir Aga, ceded to Amir Muhammad Aga al-Razzaz, also known as al-Saghir, freedman of Amir Mustafa Shurbaji al-Razzaz, 4.6/24 *qirats* in an *iltizam* in return for 2,500 *riyals* (each *riyal* worth 90 *nisf fidda* or *paras*).

In 1217/1802 the same Fatima through the same agents sold to the same man another 4/24 *qirats* in the same property in return for 500 *riyals*. Fatima thus sold *iltizams* worth 261,000 *paras* from 1773 to 1802. These were critical years and she may have needed cash. We are not told whether the money was reinvested in other properties or not. *Mahfadha* 16, *hujja* 747.

10. Zubaida Khatun, daughter of Abdallah al-Baida, freedwoman of Salun, freedwoman of Amir Husain Katkhoda Mustahfazan al-Qazdaghli, in 1188/1774 bought 4/24 of an *iltizam* from Yusif Bash Shawish Tufekjiyan, son of Abdallah, freedman of Amir Husain Effendi Katib Kabir Tufekjiyan, in return for a payment of 1,000 *riyals*. *Mahfadha* 8, *hujja* 400 bis.

11. Gulsun Khatun in 1189/1775 bought the ground rent of a property from Fatima Khatun, manumitted slave of Mustafa Bey Shahin, and Fatima Hasan Aga Gonuliyan for the sum of 150 *riyals* (13,500 *paras*). *Mahfadha* 8, *hujja* 400 bis.

Gulsun Khatun, daughter of Abdallah al-Baida, in 1217/1802 sold the usufruct to a house and 12/24 parts of another house of a waqf set up by herself and her husband, Salim Kashif, of which she was a *nazira*, in return for 540 *riyal pataques*. *Mahfadha* 16, *hujja* 756.

12. In 1210/1795 Mahbuba, daughter of Abdallah al-Baida, inherited from her deceased husband, Umar Kashif Abdallah (not to be confused with Umar Shawish Mustahfazan, also a freedman of Husain Katkhoda Mustahfazan Shaarawi), a building including four shops. *Mahfadha* 15, *hujja* 704.

13. Salun Khatun, daughter of Abdallah al-Baida, freedwoman of Bashir Aga Dar al-Saada (the chief eunuch at the Porte and guardian of the *waqfs* of the Holy Cities), in 1212/1797 bought half of a property known as Baibars field (*ghait*) plus other contiguous lands bought for the sum of 1,000 *riyals* (90,000 *nisf fidda*) to be paid at the rate of 1,100 *nisf fidda* per year. The lady lived in Medina and the transaction was carried out through her agent Burhan al-Din Ibrahim. *Mahfadha* 16, *hujja* 735.

14. Zulaikha Khatun, freedwoman of Amir Mustafa Shawish Mustahfazan al-Qazdaghli, in 1214/1799 ceded her right of 2/24 *qirats* in an *iltizam* in return for a *hulwan* of 600 *riyals* through her agent Yaqut Aga to al-Haja Suudiyya Khalifat al-Bush through her agent Masuud Aga. *Mahfadha* 16, *hujja* 755.

Zulaikha ceded her right to the usufruct in one-third of an *iltizam* to Ridwan Kashif, follower of Umar Shawish Mustahfazan, for the sum of 341 *riyals* (30,690 *paras*). Her *wakils* were her husband, Amir Sulaiman Odabasha Azaban, and her follower Jawhar Aga Abdallah.

15. Zubaida Khatun, daughter of Abdallah al-Baida, freedwoman of Mustafa Sadiq Shaikh Riwaq al-Atrak, in 1216/1801 sold 3.66/24 *qirats* of an *iltizam* to Abdal Karim Abdal Qadir Bakija, a merchant, and to Muhammad Hasan ibn Ali in return for 1,000 *riyals*. *Mahfadha* 16, *hujja* 760.

APPENDIX B
Native Elites

1. "In 1152/1739 in the presence of Muhammad, son of the deceased Haj Id the barber, and Haj Abd al-Raziq, son of Shaikh Ahmad the greengrocer, and Haj Muhammad, son of Shaikh Abd al-Raziq, and the Sharif Ali, son of al-Sayyid Sulaiman, and Hasan, son of the deceased Hajjaj al-Sharbati...the woman [al-hurma] Badra, daughter of the deceased Ismail, known as Abu Qutah, who is of sound mind and in good health, establishes of her own free will a legal waqf...comprising a property [makan] in Khutt al-Azbakiyya, as witnessed in a legal document [hujja] from the court of the Zahid mosque dated al-Hijja, 1147." The property was described as a two-story building, each floor having a door and a hal and a qaa. The property was surrounded on four sides by other properties, which were described. The property belonged to Badra, who had bought it from Hanna, son of Yusif Faraj, the Christian al-Muhandis, according to a legal document dated the second of Jamad Thani 1137, who had bought said property from the woman Muna, wife of the deceased Shaaban, according to a legal document dated 21 Rabi Awwal 1125. Having legally established Badra's right to the property, the deed stated her legal right to turn it into a waqf, which "is in perpetuity, which cannot be sold or deeded or mortgaged or exchanged or changed in any way for all eternity until the end of time." Beneficiaries of said waqf were the woman Badra during her lifetime, to live in it or rent it as she pleased and to use it in any way she pleased without anyone sharing it with her (min ghair musharik laha wa la munazi), then after her death to become a waqf in favor of her husband, al-Haj Mustafa, son of the deceased Ahmad Jalabi of the merchants (min al-tujjar) in Khutt Taht al-Rab, and the son of her sister, the deceased Atta, namely, al-Haj Abduh, son of al-Haj Muhammad Bushla, to be divided equally between the beneficiaries during their

lifetimes, then to go to their children and their children's children, etc. Badra remained the supervisor (*nazira*) over her *waqf* during her lifetime, then her heirs were to become joint supervisors of the property.

This *hujja* tells us that the woman bought the property herself, that is, she did not inherit it, although she may have inherited the money with which she bought it. It also tells us that Badra had no intention of allowing anyone other than herself to dispose of said property during her lifetime. She was to remain the *nazira* of the *waqf.* The witnesses to the deed established her or her husband as belonging to the merchant class, although not the elite of that class; they were part of the middle bourgeoisie as greengrocers and sherbet makers, though her husband seemed to be a merchant with a shop in a known street of bazaars. Shahr Aqari, no. 220, item 706, p. 489, 4 Ramadan 1152, Bab Aali.

2. Another deed dated 28 Rajab 1159/1746 was witnessed by a plethora of ulama from al-Azhar, including Shaikh Darwish, the *khatib* (preacher) of the mosque, and Shaikhs Burhan al-Din Hasan and Nur al-Din Ali, sons of the deceased Shaikh Zain al-Din Abd al-Rauf al-Halabi al-Bakri al-Siddiqi, the former *khatib* of the Azhar mosque.

Other notables were also mentioned as witnesses, but their functions were not stated. In their presence the woman Fatima, known as Tuhfa, daughter of the deceased Muhammad, son of the deceased Abdallah, son of Muhammad, son of Abdallah, son of Muhammad, son of Salih al-Zayyat (the oil seller), known as Atta, was established as the legal *wakil* (*al-wakila al-shariyya*) of the *waqf* of her grandfather according to a deed issued by the court of Qawsun on 7 Shaaban 1102. Other beneficiaries of the *waqf* were male and female relatives. The *waqf* comprised a mill (*tahuna*) with all its equipment and stables for the beasts of burden, as well as storage rooms (*manafi wa huquq*). Shahr Aqari, no. 232, item 144, p. 110, 28 Rajab 1159, Bab Aali.

3. In 1168/1754 Nafisa, daughter of Haj Abd al-Rahman, left an inheritance estimated at 481,479 *paras* (of which she had inherited 274,019 *paras* from her father), along with various amounts of coffee from the Hijaz worth 150,870 *paras*, which arrived after her father had died, but which entered the inheritance. She also possessed various items of jewelry

estimated at 56,570 *paras*. This gave a total of 481,459 *paras*; the discrepancy in the stated total may be due to a clerical error on the part of the scribe. This inheritance showed the father to be a wealthy man, who may have been among the *tujjar*, for the daughter inherited only part of that wealth, two-thirds at best. Further records show the wide variety of properties bought by women. Q.A. 167, folder 182, p. 113.

4. Halima, daughter of Haj Ahmad Ashur, in 1177/1763 bought from Khadija, daughter of al-Sayyid Muhammad al-Kayyal, the following properties (some of which Khadija had inherited from a dead sister): over 5 *qirats* in a shop and two *makans*; 5 *qirats* in a textile weaving establishment which contained ten looms, another weaving establishment (the number of looms was not mentioned), an oil-pressing establishment including machinery, a *makan* and a *hawsh*, a shop and part of a house and a flour mill; and 4/5 *qirat* of a *makan*. Q.A. 174, folder 255, pp. 126–127.

5. In 1182/1768 the inheritance of Hajia Aisha Khatun, daughter of Haj Salih Shalabi, wife of Mahmud Aga ibn Abdallah, freedman of Uthman Aga, *wakil* of Dar al-Saada, listed her properties as follows: over 7 *qirats* in three *makans*, a *rab*, a bathhouse, a building on *hikr* land, five shops, five *makans* above the preceding shops, a *wikala*, the ruins of three *makans* above the preceding *wikala*, and another *makan*. Q.A. 182, folder 287, p. 223.

6. In 1182/1768 an estate in the name of Aida Khatun, daughter of Shaikh Muhammad al-Shaarani, Shaikh Sijada of the Shaarani *tariqa* (Sufi order), declared her worth to be 70,497 *paras*, of which 4,798 *paras* were the *faiz* of an unknown area of *iltizam*; 7,452 *paras* the price of bulls and fodder, etc. The remaining sums were also the price of bulls in an *usya* and various agricultural implements such as plows and threshers. This example clearly shows that women inherited or bought *iltizams*. Q.A. 182, folder 275, pp. 211–213.

7. Fatima, daughter of Muhammad Shuaib, wife of Haj Ali Khalil al-Inbabi, left the following property in 1188/1774: 3 *qirats* and a fraction in two shops; 1 *qirat* and 4/9 *qirat* in a *maqaad* (part of a house); a little over

1 *qirat* in six businesses selling straw; over 1 *qirat* in a shop; weighing instruments deposited in one of the straw-selling establishments; over 1/2 *qirat* in two shops; less than 1 *qirat* in seven *hasils*, three floors of *wikalat al-sajai*, and three shops; and over 1 *qirat* in a shop.

Most of the property became hers in 1150/1737, which might mean that she inherited or bought it then. The witnesses to this succession were mostly *tujjar*, weighers, and shoemakers, showing that the woman's family were members of the commercial community. Q.A 125, folder 63, p. 41.

8. In 1189/1775 Fatima Abd al-Wahid al-Naqli registered the sale of half a lot (12 *qirats*) of a property held in common (*ala-lshuyu*), comprising three storage areas (*hasils*) and two floors above them, which she bought from her brother's son, Haj Hasan al-Hariri (the silk maker), for which she paid the sum of 170 *riyal pataques* or 15,300 *paras*, which she immediately turned into a *waqf*. That *waqf* established her as the *nazira*, after her the position went to her daughter, Ruqayya Abd al-Wahid, who was married to the man who had sold the property in the first place, Haj Hasan al-Hariri, and to her husband. Mahfadha 7, no. 30/31, 1189/1775.

9. In 1199/1784 Fatima Khatun, daughter of Haj Bakir Shalabi ibn Haj Hasan Qalaun al-Kabir, wife of Amir Hasan Kashif ibn Abdallah, *tabii* to the *daftardar*, left an inheritance of 3 *qirats* in a flour mill; 1/8 share in a shop; 3/4 of another mill; half a *makan*; 1/8 share in money left by her first husband, now deceased; 1/8 share in the rent of real estate previously mentioned in 1197 and 1198; 1/8 share in the produce of a garden inherited from her deceased husband; and 1/8 share of the price of various cereals coming to her from her deceased husband. Unfortunately, I have not found her previous deeds which list the other properties she owned or her husband's inheritance, which listed further properties. The deed showed a marriage between the daughter of a merchant and a mamluk amir. Q.A. 212, folder 332, pp. 236–238.

10. In 1200/1785 the inheritance for Aisha, daughter of Ali Hadaya, wife of Ali Shaarawi, left the following: half a share in two *makans*; half a share in an open area; half a share in a house; half a share in two shops; and 1 *qirat* and 9/16 *qirat* share in a *makan* and two shops. One of the shops

included the *gedik* for the shop and the instruments for a barber's establishment. All of her property was located in the Azbakiyya district, so she seems to have been interested in consolidating all her properties in one area. Q.A. 212, folder 529, p. 379.

11. In a deed dated 1211/1796 Abd al-Rahim al-Saidi, son of Najib al-Saidi, gave his wife, Fatima Abu Mahmud, the gift (*hiba*) of a house. Citadel 15, no. 712.

APPENDIX C
Women of Artisanal Classes

1. For the sake of comparison I will cite a deed that is earlier than the period studied that showed the kind of extensive property that could be left. In 1152/1739 a woman identified as the Sharifa Zainab Khatun, daughter of the deceased al-Sayyid Hasan, wife of Haj Khalil, son of the deceased Haj Ibrahim al-Ghamrawi (which tells us little about either her antecedents or her husband's or his profession, save that she was among the *ashraf*), left an inheritance estimated at 24,249 *paras*, including 3,598 *paras* for a gold bracelet, 1,101 *paras* for a silver anklet, 4,330 *paras* in coin in her husband's keeping, 1,210 *paras* in coin in her keeping, 1,000 *paras* as the price of a *makan*, and 1,100 *paras* as her back dowry. It is part of Muslim law that the back dowry be paid by the husband when the wife dies. Q.A. 148, folder 128, pp. 91–93.

2. In 1165/1751 Aisha, wife of Haj Mustafa, shaikh of the guild of coffee grinders (*daqqaqin fi-l bun*), left 10 *qirats* in a *makan*, which comprised a building and the land around it; the deed registering the acquisition of such land dated from 1153/1740, which might imply that the woman inherited or bought it twelve years earlier. Q.A. 110, folder 25, p. 11.

3. In 1166/1752 Staita, daughter of Haj Uthman al-Allaf (a dealer in fodder), wife of Haj Muhammad al-Tabbakh (the cook), together with her husband, registered property jointly owned: two separate *makans* in different areas and half a *makan* next to one of the previous two *makans*. The deed, like many other deeds, shows that marriage between individuals belonging to different guilds was just as common as the contrary, since her father dealt in fodder and her husband was a cook. Q.A. 110, folder 795, p. 342.

father dealt in fodder and her husband was a cook. Q.A. 110, folder 795, p. 342.

4. Aisha, daughter of the shaikh of the guild of weighers (*al-qabbaniyya*), wife of Shaikh Muhammad, profession unknown, left a *makan* in 1168/ 1754. Q.A. 167, folder 115, p. 68.

5. Compared to the property of the wife of the shaikh of the guild of butchers (*al-qassabin fi-l khishin*), the prior deed showed the disparity in wealth among the different artisans and their women. Aisha, wife of Abdin, left coin, gold, and silver worth 32,866 *paras* aside from the worth of her furniture, copper utensils, and other items. She had the following property: half a share (i.e., 12 *qirats*) in five *makans*, which needed rebuilding and restoring; half a share in a *makan* and 3 *qirats* and a little over in two adjacent *makans*, 12 *qirats* in a *hasil*, 3 *qirats* and a fraction in a *makan*, 3 *qirats* and a fraction in a *hawsh*, 3 *qirats* and a fraction in a *makan*, 1 *qirat* and a fraction in a *makan*, 1 *qirat* and a fraction in another *makan*, under half a *qirat* in a *wikala*, and under half a *qirat* in a *makan*. Q.A. 167, folder 2, pp. 2, 3.

6. In 1169/1755 Aida, daughter of Mustafa, former wife of Shaikh Taqi al-Din, wife or former wife of another individual identified as Ibrahim (all unknowns, since they don't rate any further descriptions of their antecedents or trades), registered 7/8 *qirat* in an oil press, 1 and 1/8 *qirats* in an adjacent flour mill, and 3/4 *qirat* in an adjacent dyeing establishment. While this was a modest inheritance, it indicates that the owner simply bought adjacent property, either for the sake of convenience or because propinquity created the opportunity to buy property. The daughter of her husband, Taqi al-Din, Shakira, left a little over 1 *qirat* in the same oil press, more than 1 *qirat* in the dyeing establishment, and over 1 *qirat* in the flour mill, indicating that the inheritance belonged to Taqi al-Din and that the widow and the daughter both inherited the property. Q.A. 182, folder 275, pp. 211, 213.

7. In another deed dated the same year Fatima, wife of Musa, probably deceased or divorced, with no mention of children, since her heirs were her

siblings, left a shop (*hanut*), 7 *qirats* and a fraction in two more shops, half a share in a shop which was a *waqf*, 6 and 3/4 *qirats* in a *makan* and two shops above it, and half a share in another shop. Q.A. 168, folder 403, p. 251.

8. Latifa, whose father was a sugar maker (*sukkari*) and who was married to a barber (*hallaq*) who was also an undertaker (*hanuti*), in 1169/1755 left an inheritance of 2 *qirats* out of 4 *qirats* in a *makan*, in a deed dated 1114/1702, which must have been inherited, and 2 *qirats* in a shop opposite the above-mentioned makan, including the furnishings and articles which were used in said shop, which Latifa had inherited from her deceased undertaker husband. Once again we note a marriage outside the guild: the daughter of a sugar maker married a barber-cum-undertaker. Q.A. 174, folder 223, p. 113.

9. Among the marriages within guilds that I came across, or at least marriages between individuals belonging to complementary guilds, we find Rumiyya, daughter of a merchant in thread, who married a dyer, Haj Gadallah. In 1176/1762 her inheritance lists a *makan* near the dyers which was registered in 1170/1756, so it may have been an inheritance, and half a full share in another *makan* registered by deeds in 1154 and 1159. That property may also have been an inheritance, or she may have bought them herself. Q.A. 174, folder 190, p. 98.

The only other marriage within a guild is that of a cook marrying the daughter of another cook.

10. In 1177/1763 Fatima, daughter of Haj Muhammad and mother of Haj Yusif al-Hariri, the silk weaver, left 19 and 1/5 *qirats* in a *makan* as well as various items including 8 dinars (*zer mahbub*), and 15 *riyals*, plus a pair of silver bracelets weighing 30 *dirhams*, all of which, minus the price of the *makan*, came to 4,708 *paras*. Q.A. 119, folder 69, pp. 32, 33.

11. Even the daughter of a lowly *saqqa* (water carrier) had property, though not very much, for in 1177/1763 Asila, daughter of Haj Zayid, the water carrier, wife of Haj Saad al-Labudi, the felt maker, left half a *makan*. She could not have inherited it from her husband because he is not referred

to as deceased. Although the father was a water carrier he, and the husband, had enough money to go on the pilgrimage, thereby rating the title "Haj." Perhaps the father was an entrepreneur in the water carrying business or was merely descended from a water carrier and practiced some other profession himself. Q.A. 174, folder 235, pp. 118–119.

12. Safiyya, daughter of a *baitar* (blacksmith), married Haj Muhammad *al-tabbakh* (the cook) and in 1182/1768 left 6 *qirats* in a *makan* and 4.5 *qirats* in another *makan*. Q.A. 122, folder 141, p. 79.

13. A couple, Aisha, daughter of a barber (*hallaq*), and her husband, a fodder merchant, together left their son a heritage of half a *makan*, which was Aisha's property, and 8 *qirats* and fractions in another *makan*, only 6 and 1/6 *qirats* of which belonged to the husband. Here we see that the daughter of a barber had more property than a feed merchant. Q.A. 122, folder 557, p. 245.

14. That same year the daughter of an iron worker or smelter (*sabbak*), who had married into the regiments since her husband was Hasan Shawish, although her son was a bathhouse keeper, left her son 2 *qirats* in a *hammam* known as Hammam al-Qazzazzin (weavers), which was registered as a *waqf* in 1173/1759, and 2 *qirats* in items for use in baths (towels, combs, bathrobes, etc.). She probably regarded a bathhouse as a lucrative investment, which indeed they were. Q.A. 182, folder 331, p. 258.

15. The daughter of a fishmonger (*sammak*), Aisha, daughter of Daud, wife of Haj Ahmad, son of Ahmad, whose trade is unlisted, left 13 *qirats* in a *makan*, plus movables worth 2,804 *paras*. Q.A. 190, folder 467, p. 384.

16. On occasion the inheritance of the spouses is listed in bulk so that one cannot distinguish the man's share from the woman's share, as in the case of a couple from the province of Qaliubiyya who, in 1189/1775, left 5 *faddans*, *gharuqa* (a form of mortgage) worth 500 *riyals*, and various other landed property (also *gharuqa*) which totaled 349 *riyals*, the land totaling 849 *riyals* or 76,410 *paras*, a nice little sum. They also left three bulls, a cow, a thresher, and two other cows co-owned with another person,

fruit trees and palm trees, plus a house and the right to till the above-mentioned property for that year. Q.A. 125, folder 409, p. 310.

These deeds indicate that only one inheritance out of twenty-two involved land which was mortgaged; all the others mentioned *makans* of various kinds, including a mill, an oil press, a dyeing establishment, a *hammam*, an undertaker's, a *hawsh*, shops, and personal goods such as coins and clothing. Out of a sampling of 116 artisans and middle to lower echelon women I have found that they invested in much the same properties as the other two strata of women. Sixty-eight women (over 58 percent), owned *makans*; twenty-four women (21 percent) owned houses; while twenty-three women (20 percent) owned shops. The only difference between the strata was that elite women owned more *iltizams*; *tujjar* and ulama women owned the same properties as the rank and file.

NOTES

Introduction

1. André Raymond, *Artisans et commerçants au Caire au XVIIIème siècle*, 2 vols. (Damascus: Institut Français de Damas, 1973), vol. 2, p. 671.

2. I owe this information to Dr. M. M. Ramadan.

Chapter 1. Women in the Eyes of Men: Myth and Reality

1. Sharon W. Tiffany, ed., *Women and Society* (Montreal, 1979), p. 2.

2. Jack Goody, *Production and Reproduction* (Cambridge: Cambridge University Press, 1976), p. 35.

3. *Zawj* in Quran 4:1 passim and quotation in 3:195.

4. Fatma Mernissi, *Le Harem politique* (Paris, 1987), p. 158.

5. Quran 4:34.

6. Mernissi, *Le Harem politique*, p. 158; Leila Ahmad, *Women and Gender in Islam* (New Haven: Yale University Press, 1992); Barbara Stowasser, *Women in the Qur'an, Traditions, and Interpretation* (New York: Oxford University Press, 1994).

7. Quran 33:53.

8. Nabia Abbott, *Two Queens of Bagdad* (Chicago, 1946), p. 91.

9. Ibid.; see Part II, pp. 137ff.

10. Stanford Shaw, *History of the Ottoman Empire and Modern Turkey*, 2 vols. (Cambridge, 1976, 1977), vol. 1, p. 179.

11. Cynthia Nelson, "Public and Private Politics: Women in the Middle Eastern World," *American Ethnologist* 1 (1974): 551–563.

12. Jonathan Berkey, "Women and Islamic Education," in *Women in Middle Eastern History*, ed. Nikki Keddie and Beth Baron (New Haven: Yale University Press, 1992), p. 151.

13. A. al-Sayyid Marsot, "The Political and Economic Functions of the Ulama in the Eighteenth Century," *Journal of the Social and Economic History of the Orient* 16, nos. 2–3 (1973): 130–154.

14. Philippe Fargues, "Explosion démographique ou rupture sociale?" in *Democracy without Democrats*, ed. Ghassan Salame (London: I. B. Tauris, 1993); also *Démocraties sans démocrates* (Paris: Fayard, 1994), Chapter 4, pp. 163–197.

Chapter 2. Political Struggles: The Search for Leadership

1. André Raymond, *Artisans et commerçants au Caire au XVIIIème siècle*, vol. 2, pp. 692ff.

2. Jean Deny, *Sommaire des archives turques du Caire* (Cairo: Société Royale de Géographie d'Egypte, 1930), pp. 42ff.

3. Stanford Shaw, *Ottoman Egypt in the Age of the French Revolution*, Harvard Middle Eastern Monograph Series (Cambridge, Mass.: Harvard University Press, 1964), p. 78.

4. A. B. Clot Bey, *Aperçu général sur L'Egypte*, 2 vols. (Brussels, 1840), vol. 2, pp. 340–341.

5. Shaw, *Ottoman Egypt in the Age of the French Revolution*, pp. 37, 80, 82.

6. Ahmad Shalabi Abd al-Ghani, *Awdah al-isharat fi man tawalla Misr al-Qahira min al-wuzara wa-l bashat*, ed. Abd al-Rahim A. Abd al-Rahim (Cairo, 1978), p. 482. He wrote that Muhammad Bey Charkas had one thousand *kis* a year, the *kis* being 20,000 *paras*.

7. Abd al-Rahim A. Abd al-Rahim, *Al-rif al-Misri fi-l qarn al-thamin ashr* (Cairo, 1974), p. 75.

8. Ibid., p. 95.

9. Fred Lawson, *The Social Origins of Egyptian Expansionism during the Muhammad Ali Period* (New York: Columbia University Press, 1992), pp. 25, 27.

10. Abd al-Rahim, *Al-rif al-Misri*, p. 89.

11. Raymond, *Artisans*, vol. 2, pp. 652ff., 815.

12. Abd al-Rahman al-Jabarti, *Ajaib al-athar fi-l tarajim wa-l akhbar*, 4 vols. (Cairo, 1882), vol. 1, p. 203.

13. See Raymond, *Artisans*, Chapter 3.

14. Shaw, *Ottoman Egypt in the Age of the French Revolution*, p. 50.

15. Abd al-Rahim, *Al-rif al-Misri*, p. 96.

16. Ibid., p. 88. For a comparison of landholding with earlier and later periods, see ibid. and Ali Barakat, *Tatawwur al-mulkiyya al-ziraiyya fi Misr: 1813–1914* (Cairo, 1977).

17. Albert Hourani, "The Syrians in Egypt in the Eighteenth and Nineteenth Centuries," in *Colloque international sur l'histoire du Caire* (East Berlin, 1969), p. 222. Also Raymond, *Artisans*, vol. 2, pp. 483ff.

18. Albert Hourani, *The Emergence of the Modern Middle East* (Berkeley, 1981), p. 40.

19. Jabarti, *Ajaib*, vol. 2, p. 79.

20. Raymond, *Artisans*, vol. 1, p. 101.

21. Ibid.; also Marcel Clerget, *Le Caire* (Cairo, 1924).

22. Jabarti, *Ajaib*, vol. 2, p. 191.

23. Ibid., p. 195.

24. Ibid., pp. 238–239.

25. Raymond, *Artisans*, vol. 1, p. 43. See Table 1 above.

26. Victor Nee, "A Theory of Market Transition," *American Sociological Review* 54, no. 5 (October 1989): 666.

Chapter 3. Society in Mamluk Egypt: The Elites

1. Abd al-Wahhab Bakr, "Al-ilaqat al-ijtimaiyya fi Misr al-Uthmaniyya," in *Al-hayat al-ijtimaiyya fi-l wilayat al-Arabiyya athna al-ahd al-Uthmani*, ed. Abd al-Jelil al-Temimi (Zaghouan: 1988), p. 165, passim.

2. I am most grateful to Nelly Hanna, who has supplied me with much of the information regarding the contents of marriage contracts found in the Mahkama Shariyya archives. She is at present working on a project involving such contracts.

3. Jack Goody, *Production and Reproduction* (Cambridge: Cambridge University Press, 1976), p. 13.

4. Ibid., p. 35.

5. Carl Petry, "Class Solidarity versus Gender Gain," in *Women in Middle Eastern History*, ed. Nikki Keddie and Beth Baron (New Haven: Yale University Press, 1992), p. 134.

6. Ibid., p. 133, referring to M. M. Amin, *Catalogue des documents d'archives du Caire* (Cairo: Institut d'Archéologie Orientale du Caire, 1981).

7. Ian C. Dengler, "Turkish Women in the Ottoman Empire: The Classical Age," in *Women in the Muslim World*, ed. L. Beck and N. Keddie (Cambridge, Mass.: Harvard University Press, 1978), pp. 236–237.

8. Nelly Hanna, *Habiter au Caire* (Cairo: Institut Français d'Archéologie Orientale du Caire, 1991), pp. 42–43, 73–74, 75, 141.

9. Ibid., pp. 42, 158: "a tendency in palaces belonging to the military to constitute autonomous entities which are self-sufficient regarding the needs of daily life."

10. Ibid., pp. 50–51.

11. Ibid., p. 74.

12. A. B. Clot Bey, *Aperçu général sur L'Egypte*, vol. 2, p. 395: "In Europe it is generally imagined that the harem is a kind of place of prostitution, the exclusive theatre of the most numerous sexual pleasures and stultifying debauchery of a people sapped by libertinage. One errs; a severe order, a rigorous decency, reign in the harem, and make it, in many ways, similar to our monastic establishments."

13. Goody, *Production and Reproduction*, p. 114.

14. C. Lévi-Strauss, *The Elementary Structures of Kinship*, ed. Rodney Needham (Boston: Beacon Press, 1969), pp. 480–481.

15. Abd al-Rahman al-Jabarti, *Ajaib al-athar fi-l tarajim wa-l akhbar*, vol. 2, p. 3.

16. Ibid., vol. 1, p. 206.

17. Ibid., p. 251.

18. Ibid., p. 412.

19. Ibid., vol. 2, p. 223.

20. Ibid., pp. 17, 206.

21. Ibid., vol. 4, p. 264; also Daniel Crecelius, *The Roots of Modern Egypt: A Study of the Regimes of Ali Bey al-Kabir and Muhammad Bey Abu al-Dhahab: 1760–1775* (Chicago, 1982), p. 117.

22. Ibid.

23. Jabarti, *Ajaib*, vol. 2, p. 20.

24. Ibid., vol. 3, pp. 197–198.

25. Ibid., p. 268.

26. Ibid., vol. 2, p. 58.

27. Ibid., vol. 1, pp. 251–252.

28. I have opted to use the spelling for Qazdaghli recommended by Jane Hathaway in "Sultans, Pashas, Taqwims and Muhimmes," in *Eighteenth Century Egypt: The Arabic Manuscript Sources*, ed. Daniel Crecelius (Claremont: Regina Books, 1990). I have used the incorrect Egyptian transliteration "Hanum"—the term used by the Arabic historiographers—instead of the correct Ottoman "Khanum." Hanum and Khatun are used interchangeably.

29. Ibid., p. 206. See also David Ayalon, "Studies in al-Jabarti," in *Studies on the Mamluks of Egypt* (London: Variorum Reprints, 1977), p. 284. Ayalon wrongly describes Uthman as having "mistreated his wife," whereas Jabarti writes *zawjat sayyidih* (his master's wife).

30. See ibid, vol. 2, pp. 117ff., for details of that incident.

31. Clot Bey, *Aperçu*, p. 97: "Women exert great authority. More than one political incident was triggered in the mysteries of the harem. . . . The power women exert over their husbands is often put to good use. Muslim ladies meet without hindrance and it is during their visits that they ask for reciprocal favors for their husbands and their families, favors which, knowing the influence they enjoy over their masters, the women know they can obtain through willing submission."

32. Jabarti, *Ajaib*, vol. 4, p. 264.

33. Clot Bey, *Aperçu*, p. 398.

34. Jabarti, *Ajaib*, vol. 2, p. 195.

35. Daniel Crecelius, "Incidence of Waqf Cases in Three Cairo Courts: 1640–1802," *Journal of the Economic and Social History of the Orient* 29, no. 2 (June 1986): 189.

36. Ibid., p. 186.

37. Ibid., p. 181.

38. Hanna, *Habiter au Caire*, p. 35.

39. See Appendix A.

40. I owe this information to Dr. Terry Walz.

41. Jabarti, *Ajaib*, vol. 4, p. 264.

42. Qisma Askariyya, no. 113, folder 190, item no. 6578, p. 472.

43. *Mahfadha* 7, hujja 8.

44. *Mahfadha* 16, hujja 773.

45. Hanna, *Habiter au Caire*, p. 28.

46. Ibid., p. 61.

47. *Mahfadha* 7, *hujjas* 321, 331, 332, 333; *mahfadha* 10, *hujjas* 453, 455, 458, 464, 480, 492; *mahfadha* 15, hujjas 693, 70; *mahfadha* 16, *hujjas* 736, 767. André Raymond, *Artisans et commerçants au Caire au XVIIIème siècle*, has given the following references, vol. 2, pp. 715–716: Citadel V, 492, 1785; VI, 554, 1788; VII, 604 and 617, 1791; VIII, 656, 1793; 781, 1797; X, 7887, 1802.

48. Raymond, *Artisans*, vol. 2, pp. 715ff.

49. Jabarti, *Ajaib*, vol. 2, pp. 219–221.

50. Ibid., vol. 3, p. 16.

51. Abd al-Rahim A. Abd al-Rahim, "Land Tenure in Egypt and Its Social Effects on Egyptian Society: 1798–1813," in *Land Tenure and Social Transformation in the Middle East*, ed. Tarif Khalidi (Beirut: American University in Beirut, 1984), p. 241.

52. Ibid.

53. Nelly Hanna, *An Urban History of Bulaq in the Mamluk and Ottoman Periods* (Cairo: Annales Islamologiques, 1983), p. 57.

54. Jabarti, *Ajaib*, vol. 3, pp. 295–296.

55. Abd al-Rahim, "Land Tenure," p. 241.

56. Jabarti, *Ajaib*, vol. 4, p. 264.

57. Ibid., vol. 3, pp. 295–296.

58. Afaf Lutfi al-Sayyid Marsot, "A Socio-economic Sketch of the Ulama," in *Colloque international sur l'histoire du Caire* (East Berlin, 1969), p. 317; also same author, "The Political and Economic Functions of the Ulama in the Eighteenth Century," *Journal of the Economic and Social History of the Orient* 16, nos. 2–3 (1973): 152ff.

59. E. M. Chaney and M. Schmink, "Women and Modernization, Access to Tools," in *Sex and Class in Latin America*, ed. June Nash and Helen I. Safa (New York: Praeger, 1976), p. 163.

Chapter 4. Indigenous Elites in the Eighteenth Century: Ulama and Tujjar

1. Abd al-Rahman al-Jabarti, *Ajaib al-athar fi-l tarajim wa-l akhbar*, 4 vols. (Cairo, 1882), vol. 1, pp. 8ff. Maqrizi was a medieval writer who wrote extensively on the mamluks of the earlier period. Much of Jabarti's work that deals with the period earlier than 1776 was derived from the Damurdash Chronicles. See the interesting article on the subject by Daniel Crecelius, "Ahmad Shalabi ibn Abd al-Ghani and Ahmad Katkhuda Azaban al-Damurdashi: Two Sources for al-Jabarti's *Ajaib al-Akhbar fi-l Tarajim wa-l Akhbar*," in *Eighteenth Century Egypt: The Arabic Manuscript Sources*, ed. Daniel Crecelius (Claremont: Regina Books, 1990), pp. 89–102.

See also the article by George Makdisi, "Authority in the Islamic Community," in *La Notion d'autorité au Moyen Age: Islam, Byzance, Occident*, ed. G. Makdisi (Paris: Presses Universitaires de France, 1982), pp. 117ff.

2. Afaf Lutfi al-Sayyid Marsot, "A Socio-economic Sketch of the Ulama," in *Colloque international sur l'histoire du Caire*, p. 317; and the same author, "Political and Economic Functions of the Ulama in the Eighteenth Century," *Journal of the Social and Economic History of the Orient* 16, nos. 2–3 (1973): 153; André Raymond, *Artisans et commerçants au Caire au XVIIIème siècle*, vol. 2, p. 428.

3. Marsot, "Functions," p. 149.

4. Marsot, "Socio-economic Sketch," p. 317.

5. Raymond, *Artisans*, vol. 2, p. 429.

6. Marsot, "Functions," p. 147

7. Ali Pasha Mubarak, *Al-Khitat al-Tawfiqiyya al-jadida li Misr al-Qahira*, 20 vols. (Cairo, 1305/1887), vol. 14, p. 35. There were three villages bearing that name.

8. Marsot, "Socio-economic Sketch," p. 318.

9. Comte Estève, "Mémoire sur les finances d'Egypte," in *Description de l'Egypte: Etat moderne*, 2d ed., 30 vols. (Paris, 1882), vol. 12, p. 222.

10. Jabarti, *Ajaib*, vol. 1, pp. 186–188, 191–192.

11. Ibid., 304.

12. Ibid., vol. 4, pp. 233ff.

13. Nelly Hanna, *An Urban History of Bulaq in the Mamluk and Ottoman Periods*, p. 48.

14. Nelly Hanna, *Construction Work in Ottoman Cairo* (Cairo, 1984), pp. 35–37.

15. Jabarti, *Ajaib*, vol. 2, p. 260.

16. Marsot, "Functions," p. 153.

17. Jabarti, *Ajaib*, vol. 4, p. 161.

18. Marsot, "Functions," p. 153.

19. Jabarti, *Ajaib*, vol. 1, pp. 385ff.

20. Nabia Abbott, *Two Queens of Bagdad* (Chicago, 1946), p. 140.

21. Qisma Askariyya (hereafter cited as Q.A.), 167, folder 170, p. 106.

22. Q.A. 168, folder 423, p. 261.

23. Cited in Hanna, *Urban History*, p. 14.

24. Jabarti, *Ajaib*, vol. 1, p. 204.

25. Raymond, *Artisans*, vol. 2, pp. 408–409.

26. Jabarti, *Ajaib*, vol. 1, p. 204.

27. Q.A. 137, pp. 106–107; also 203, pp. 157 and 182.

28. Jabarti, *Ajaib*, vol. 1, pp. 87, 204. Muhammad al-Sharaibi al-Kabir was not related to Muhammad Dada al-Sharaibi, who took his surname as his heir and partner. Thus Ahmad Shalabi, son of Muhammad, married Amina, daughter of Muhammad Dada, and not her uncle, as Raymond erroneously states (*Artisans*, vol. 2, p. 412).

29. Raymond, Artisans, vol. 2, p. 412.

30. Mahkamat al-Bab al-AAli, hujja 244, item 169, p. 178.

31. Terry Walz, *Trade between Egypt and Bilad al-Sudan* (Cairo: Institut Français d'Archéologie Orientale du Caire, 1978), p. 115n2.

32. Raymond, *Artisans*, vol. 2, p. 405.

33. Jabarti, *Ajaib*, vol. 2, p. 58.

34. Ibid., p. 221; also Raymond, *Artisans*, vol. 2, p. 786.

35. See Chapter 3 above.

36. Abd al-Rahman Abdul Tawab and André Raymond, "La Waqfiyya de Mustafa Gaafar," *Annales Islamologiques* 14 (1978): 178–194.

37. Ibid., p. 184.

38. Jabarti, *Ajaib*, vol. 2, p. 18. See the discussion of Yusif Bey above.

39. See Chapter 3 above.

40. Jabarti, *Ajaib*, vol. 2, p. 139, and vol. 4, p. 271.

41. For information regarding Ottoman women, see Fanny Davis, *The Ottoman Lady: A Social History from 1718–1918* (New York: Greenwood Press, 1986).

42. Jabarti, Ajaib, vol. 2, p. 140.

43. See Billie Melman, *Women's Orients: English Women and the Middle East, 1718–1918* (London, 1992).

44. Jabarti, *Ajaib*, vol. 3, p. 140.

45. Ibid., p. 196.

46. Ibid., vol. 2, p. 97.

47. *Mahfadha* 7, 1193/1779.

48. Q.A. 1774.

49. Peter Gran, *Islamic Roots of Capitalism* (Austin: University of Texas Press, 1979), p. 51.

50. Q.A. 174, folder 103, p. 58.

51. Q.A. 174, folder 181, p. 92.

52. Q.A. 204, folder 256, p. 189.

53. Hanna, *Urban History*, p. 9.

Chapter 5. Artisans and Ayan: Urban and Rural Middle and Lower Classes in the Eighteenth Century

1. Nelly Hanna, *An Urban History of Bulaq in the Mamluk and Ottoman Periods*, pp. 16ff.

2. André Raymond, *Artisans et commerçants au Caire au XVIIIème siècle*, p. 380, quoting Maqrizi.

3. Nicolas Turc, *Chronique d'Egypte: 1789–1804*, p. 45 French/p. 31 Arabic.

4. M. de Chabrol, "Essai sur les moeurs des habitans modernes de l'Egypte," in *Description de l'Egypte: Etat moderne* (Paris, 1882), p. 438; Raymond, *Artisans*, vol. 2, p. 387.

5. Cited in Abd al-Rahman al-Jabarti, *Ajaib al-athar fi-l tarajim wa-l akhbar*, vol. 1, 104.

6. Hanna, *Urban History*, p. 16.

7. Raymond, *Artisans*, vol. 1, p. 205.

8. Ibid., vol. 2, p. 374.

9. Ibid., p. 376.

10. Ibid., p. 42.

11. Ibid., pp. 377–378.

12. Chabrol, "Essai," p. 423, Raymond, *Artisans*, vol. 2, p. 385.

13. Raymond, *Artisans*, vol. 2, pp. 386ff.

14. Daniel Crecelius, "Damiette in the Late Eighteenth Century," *Journal of the American Research Centre in Egypt* 27 (1990): 187n13.

15. Ibid., p. 188.

16. Ibid., p. 189.

17. Raymond, *Artisans*, vol. 2, p. 815.

18. Fred Lawson, *The Social Origins of Egyptian Expansionism during the Muhammad Ali Period*, p. 25.

19. Lawson, *Social Origins*, Chapter 2, especially p. 21.

20. Raymond, *Artisans*, vol. 2, pp. 576–577.

21. Engin Deniz Akarli, "Uses of Law among Istanbul Artisans and Tradesmen" (forthcoming), p. 2.

22. Ibid., p. 5.

23. Halil Inalcik, *The Ottoman Empire* (New York: Praeger, 1973), p. 160.

24. Ian C. Dengler, "Turkish Women in the Ottoman Empire: The Classical Age," in *Women in the Muslim World,* ed. L. Beck and N. Keddie, p. 230.

25. Ilamat 44, p. 2, no. 6, Shaaban 1866. I owe this information and reference to Dr. Terry Walz.

26. Hanna, *Urban History,* pp. 45, 59.

27. Ibid., p. 73.

28. Chabrol, "Essai," pp. 516–517, Raymond, *Artisans,* vol. 2, pp. 386–387.

29. Edward William Lane, *Manners and Customs of the Modern Egyptians,* 2 vols. (London: 1849; 1st ed. 1836), vol. 1, p. 38.

30. Ibid, vol. 1, p. 266.

31. Nicolas Turc, *Chronique d'Egypte: 1798–1804,* p. 45 French/p. 31 Arabic.

32. Raymond, *Artisans,* vol. 2, p. 388.

33. See Table 3 and Appendix C.

34. Raymond, *Artisans,* vol. 2, 389–390.

35. Lane, *Manners and Customs,* p. 247.

36. Ibid., p. 267.

37. Raymond, *Artisans,* vol. 2, p. 379.

38. Hanna, *Habiter au Caire,* p. 158: "The strict segregation [of sexes] practiced during certain periods in the large residences of the dominant class is not apparent in average[-sized] or modest houses."

39. Ibid., p. 151.

40. Ibid., p. 149: "The elements one finds in the average house indicate that to the contrary the occupants, for various needs, had recourse to the outside."

41. Abd al-Wahhab Bakr, "Al-ilaqat al-ijtimaiyya fi Misr al-Uthmaniyya," in *Al-hayat al-ijtimaiyya fi-l wilayat al-Arabiyya athna al-ahd al-Uthmani,* ed. Abd al-Jelil al-Temimi (Zaghouan: 1988), pp. 157–159.

42. Ibid., p. 157.

43. Ronald Jennings, "Women in Early Seventeenth Century Ottoman Judicial Records: The Sharia Court of Anatolia and Kayseri," *Journal of the Social and Economic History of the Orient* 18, no. 1: 65.

44. Both this and the following account were given to me orally by Dr. Hanna, for which I am most grateful. They can also be found in N. Hanna, "The Administration of Courts in Ottoman Cairo," in *The State and Its Servants: Administration in Egypt in the Sixteenth–Twentieth Centuries,* ed. N. Hanna (Cairo, forthcoming).

45. N. J. Coulson, *A History of Islamic Law* (Edinburgh, 1964), p. 199; David Pearl, *A Textbook on Islamic Law* (London: Croom Helm, 1979), p. 109.

46. Hanna, *Urban History,* p. 27.

47. Ahmad Shalabi Abd al-Ghani, *Awdah al-isharat fi man tawalla Misr al-Qahira min al-wuzara wa-l bashat,* annotated by Abd al-Rahim A. Abd al-Rahim (Cairo, 1978), p. 111.

48. Turc, *Chronique,* p. 45 French/p. 31 Arabic.

49. See Chapter 3 above.

50. Jabarti, *Ajaib,* vol. 1, p. 203.

51. Ibrahim el-Mouelhy, *Le Paysan d'Egypte à travers l'histoire* (Cairo, 1954), pp. 44–47.

52. Abd al-Rahim A. Abd al-Rahim, "Hazz al-Quhuf," *Journal of the Social and Economic History of the Orient* 1 (January 1975). Baer gave his interpretation in a lecture at UCLA.

53. See Ken Cuno, "Egypt's Wealthy Peasantry," in *Land Tenure and Social Transformation in the Middle East,* ed. Tarif Khalidi (Beirut, 1984), p. 324.

54. Judith Tucker, *Women in Nineteenth-Century Egypt* (Cambridge: Cambridge University Press, 1985), p. 44.

55. Ken Cuno, "Commercial Relations between Town and Village in Eighteenth Century and Early Nineteenth Century Egypt," *Annales Islamologiques* 24 (1988): 111–136.

56. See Lawson, Social Origins; and Afaf Lutfi al-Sayyid Marsot, *Egypt in the Reign of Muhammad Ali* (Cambridge: Cambridge University Press, 1984), pp. 132ff.

57. Afaf Lutfi al-Sayyid Marsot, "The Political and Economic Functions of the Ulama in the Eighteenth Century," *Journal of the Economic and Social History of the Orient* 16, nos. 2–3 (1973): 133.

58. Jabarti, *Ajaib,* vol. 3, p. 28.

Chapter 6. The Nineteenth Century: The Advent of Centralization

1. Judith Tucker, *Women in Nineteenth-Century Egypt,* p. 130. I am grateful to Christine Ahmed, who helped me rethink and tighten the argument in this chapter.

2. Haim Gerber, *The Social Origins of the Modern Middle East* (London, 1987).

3. Sherry Vatter, "A City Divided: A Socio-economic History of Damascus, Syria 1840–1880" (Ph.D. dissertation, UCLA, forthcoming).

4. Tucker, *Women,* p. 86.

5. E. R. J. Owen, *The Middle East in the World Economy,* (London: Methuen, 1981), p. 76.

6. Juan R. I. Cole, *Colonialism and Revolution in the Middle East: Social and Cultural Origins of Egypt's Urabi Movement* (Princeton: Princeton University Press, 1993).

7. *Mémoires de Nubar Pacha*, ed. Mirrit Ghali (Beirut, 1983), pp. 71ff.

8. Ali Barakat, *Tatawwur al-mulkiyya al-ziraiyya fi Misr: 1813–1914* (Cairo, 1977), pp. 71ff.

9. Ibid., pp. 37ff.; also pp. 101ff.

10. Ibid., p. 103.

11. Maha Ghalwash, Ph.D. dissertation, Princeton University (personal communication).

12. Ken Cuno, review of Tucker book in *Jusur* 4 (1988): 81.

13. Ghalwash personal communication.

14. Jeffrey Collins, *The Egyptian Elite under Cromer: 1882–1907* (Berlin, 1984), pp. 117–118.

15. Henry Salt in Cuno, "Egypt's Wealthy Peasantry," in *Land Tenure and Social Transformation in the Middle East*, ed. Tarif Khalidi, p. 496.

16. Tucker, *Women*, p. 89.

17. A. A. al-Hitta, *Tarikh al-Zira a al-Misriyya fi ahd Muhammad Ali al-Kabir* (Cairo, 1950), p. 72.

18. Afaf Lutfi al-Sayyid Marsot, *Egypt in the Reign of Muhammad Ali*, p. 137.

19. Barakat, *Tatawwur*, p. 491.

20. Ibid., pp. 501ff.

21. Marsot, *Muhammad Ali*, p. 169.

22. Cuno, review in *Jusur*, p. 77.

23. Collins, *Egyptian Elite*.

24. Charles Issawi, *The Economic History of the Middle East: 1800–1914* (Chicago: University of Chicago Press, 1975), p. 38.

25. Gabriel Baer, *Egyptian Guilds in Modern Times* (Jerusalem, 1964), p. 139.

26. Owen, *Middle East*, p. 88.

27. David Landes, *Bankers and Pashas* (Cambridge, Mass.: Harvard University Press, 1958).

28. Pierre Crabitès, *Ismail the Maligned Khedive* (London: George Routledge and Sons, 1933).

29. Owen, *Middle East*, p. 74.

30. Tucker, *Women*, p. 83.

31. Ibid., p. 89.

32. Ibid., pp. 90, 101.

33. Nelly Hanna, *An Urban History of Bulaq in the Mamluk and Ottoman Periods*.

34. Marsot, *Muhammad Ali*, pp. 75ff.

35. See Leila Ahmad, *Women and Gender in Islam*, pp. 155–164, re Amin. Also Beth Baron, "The Rise of a New Literary Culture: The Women's Press in Egypt" (Ph.D. dissertation, University of California, Los Angeles, 1988).

36. L. J. Nicholson, *Gender and History: The Limits of Social Theory in the Age of the Family* (New York: Columbia University Press, 1986), p. 43.

37. Ibid., p. 45.

38. Bridget Hill, *Women, Work, and Sexual Politics in Eighteenth-Century England* (Oxford: Blackwell, 1989).

39. E. M. Chaney and M. Schmink, "Women and Modernization, Access to Tools," in June Nash and Helen I. Safa, *Sex and Class in Latin America*, pp. 163, 167, 176.

SELECT BIBLIOGRAPHY

Primary Sources in Arabic
Citadel archives (*mahfadha*)
Qisma archives (Qisma Arabiyya and Qisma Askariyya)
Shahr al-Aqari archives

Secondary Sources
Abd al-Ghani, Ahmad Shalabi. *Awdah al-isharat fi man tawalla Misr al-Qahira min al-wuzara wa-l bashat.* Annotated by Abd al-Rahim A. Abd al-Rahim. Cairo, 1978.
Abd al-Rahim, Abd al-Rahim A. "Hazz al-Quhuf." *Journal of the Economic and Social History of the Orient* 1 (January 1975).
————."Land Tenure in Egypt and Its Social Effects on Egyptian Society: 1798–1813." In *Land Tenure and Social Transformation in the Middle East*, ed. Tarif Khalidi. Beirut: American University in Beirut, 1984.
Abdul Tawab, Abd al-Rahman, and André Raymond. "La Waqfiyya de Mustafa Gaafar." *Annales Islamologiques* 14 (1978): 178–194.
Abu Zahra, Shaikh M. *Ahkam al-tarikat wa-l mawarith.* Cairo: Dar al-Fikr al-Arabi, 1963.
Ahmad, Leila. *Women and Gender in Islam.* New Haven: Yale University Press, 1992.
Akarli, Engin Deniz. "Uses of Law among Istanbul Artisans and Tradesmen." Forthcoming.
Ayalon, David. *Studies on the Mamluks of Egypt.* London: Variorum Reprints, 1977.
Bakr, Abd al-Wahhab. "Al-ilaqat al-ijtimaiyya fi Misr al-Uthmaniyya." In *Al-hayat al-ijtimaiyya fi-l wilayat al-Arabiyya athna al-ahd al-Uthmani.* ed. Abd al-Jelil al-Temimi. Zaghouan, 1988.
Barakat, Ali. *Tatawwur al-mulkiyya al-ziraiyya fi Misr: 1813–1914.* Cairo, 1977.
Chabrol, M de. "Essai sur les moeurs des habitans modernes de l'Egypte." In *Description de l'Egypte: Etat moderne.* 20 vols. Paris, 1882.
Chaney, E. M., and M. Schmink. "Women and Modernization, Access to Tools."

In *Sex and Class in Latin America,* ed. June Nash and Helen I. Safa. New York: Praeger, 1976.

Clerget, Marcel. *Le Caire.* Cairo: Imprimerie E. and R. Schindler, 1924.

Clot Bey, A. B. *Aperçu général sur l'Egypte.* 2 vols. Brussels: Meline and Cans, 1840.

Cole, Juan R. I. *Colonialism and Revolution in the Middle East: Social and Cultural Origins of Egypt's Urabi Movement.* Princeton: Princeton University Press, 1993.

Coontz, S., and P. Henderson. "Property Forms, Political Power and Female Labour." In *Women's Work, Men's Property: The Origins of Gender and Class,* ed. S. Coontz and P. Henderson. London, 1986.

Crecelius, Daniel. "Damiette in the Late Eighteenth Century." Journal of the American Research Centre in Egypt 27 (1990): 185–195

———, ed. *Eighteenth Century Egypt: The Arabic Manuscript Sources.* Claremont: Regina Books, 1990.

———. "Incidence of Waqf Cases in Three Cairo Courts: 1640–1802." *Journal of the Economic and Social History of the Orient* 29, no. 2 (June 1986): 176–189.

———. *The Roots of Modern Egypt: A Study of the Regimes of Ali Bey al-Kabir and Muhammad Bey Abu al-Dhahab: 1760–1775.* Chicago, 1982.

Cuno, Ken. "Commercial Relations between Town and Village in Eighteenth Century and Early Nineteenth Century Egypt." *Annales Islamologiques* 24 (1988): 111–136.

———. "Egypt's Wealthy Peasantry." In *Land Tenure and Social Transformation in the Middle East,* ed. Tarif Khalidi. Beirut: American University in Beirut, 1984.

———. *The Pasha's Peasants.* Cambridge: Cambridge University Press, 1992.

———. Review of Tucker book in *Jusur* 4 (1988): 81.

Davis, Fanny. *The Ottoman Lady: A Social History from 1718–1918.* New York: Greenwood Press, 1986.

Dengler, Ian C. "Turkish Women in the Ottoman Empire: The Classical Age." In *Women in the Muslim World,* ed. L. Beck and N. Keddie. Cambridge, Mass.: Harvard University Press, 1978.

Deny, Jean. *Sommaire des archives turques du Caire.* Cairo: Société Royale de Géographie d'Egypte, 1930.

Estève, Comte. "Mémoire sur les finances d'Egypte." In *Description de l'Egypte: Etat moderne.* 2d ed. Paris, 1882.

Gibb, H. A. R., and Harold Bowen. *Islamic Society and the West.* 2 vols. Oxford, 1956.

Gran, Peter. *Islamic Roots of Capitalism.* Austin: University of Texas Press, 1979.

Hanna, Nelly. *Construction Work in Ottoman Cairo.* Cairo, 1984.

————. *Habiter au Caire.* Cairo: Institut Français d'Archéologie Orientale du Caire, 1992.

————. *An Urban History of Bulaq in the Mamluk and Ottoman Periods.* Cairo: Annales Islamologiques, 1983.

Hathaway, Jane. "Sultans, Pashas, Taqwims and Muhimmes." In *Eighteenth Century Egypt: The Arabic Manuscript Sources,* ed. Daniel Crecelius. Claremont: Regina Books, 1990.

Hill, Bridget. *Women, Work, and Sexual Politics in Eighteenth-Century England.* Oxford: Blackwell, 1989.

al-Hitta, A. A. *Tarikh al-Zira a al-Misriyya fi ahd Muhammad Ali al-Kabir.* Cairo, 1950.

Hourani, Albert. "The Syrians in Egypt in the Eighteenth and Nineteenth Centuries." In *Colloque International sur l'histoire du Caire,* pp. 221–283. East Berlin, 1969.

Inalcik, Halil. *The Ottoman Empire.* New York: Praeger, 1973.

Issawi, Charles. *The Economic History of the Middle East: 1800–1914.* Chicago: University of Chicago Press, 1966.

Al-Jabarti, Abd al-Rahman. *Ajaib al-athar fi-l tarajim wa-l akhbar.* 4 vols. Cairo, 1882.

Jennings, Ronald. "Women in Early Seventeenth Century Ottoman Judicial Records: The Sharia Courts of Anatolia and Kayseri." *Journal of the Economic and Social History of the Orient* 18, no. 1.

Lane, Edward William. *Manners and Customs of the Modern Egyptians.* 2 vols. London, 1849 (1st ed. 1836).

Lawson, Fred. *The Social Origins of Egyptian Expansionism during the Muhammad Ali Period.* New York: Columbia University Press, 1992.

Makdisi, George. "Authority in the Islamic Community." In *La Notion d'autorité au Moyen Age: Islam, Byzance, Occident,* ed. G. Makdisi. Paris: Presses Universitaires de France, 1982.

Mernissi, Fatma. *Le Harem politique.* Paris, 1987.

el-Mouelhy, Ibrahim. *Le Paysan d'Egypte à travers l'histoire.* Cairo, 1954.

Mubarak, Ali Pasha. *Al-Khitat al-Tawfiqiyya al-jadida li Misr al-Qahira.* 20 vols. Cairo, 1305/1887.

Nee, Victor. "A Theory of Market Transition." *American Sociological Review* 54, no. 5 (October 1989).

Raymond, André. *Artisans et commerçants au Caire au XVIIIème siècle.* 2 vols. Damascus: Institut Français de Damas, 1973.

Sami, Amin. *Taqwim al-Nil.* Cairo, 1939.

al-Sayyid Marsot, Afaf Lutfi. *Egypt in the Reign of Muhammad Ali.* Cambridge: Cambridge University Press, 1984.

———. "The Political and Economic Functions of the Ulama in the Eighteenth Century." *Journal of the Economic and Social History of the Orient* 16, nos. 2–3 (1973): 130–154.

———. "A Socio-economic Sketch of the Ulama." In *Colloque international sur l'histoire du Caire.* East Berlin, 1969.

———. "The Ulama of Cairo in the Eighteenth and Nineteenth Centuries." In *Scholars, Saints and Sufis,* ed. N. Keddie. Berkeley: University of California Press, 1972.

Shaw, Stanford. *Ottoman Egypt in the Age of the French Revolution.* Cambridge, Mass.: Harvard University Press, 1964.

———. *Ottoman Egypt in the Eighteenth Century.* Harvard Middle Eastern Monograph Series. Cambridge, Mass.: Harvard University Press, 1962.

Tucker, Judith. *Women in Nineteenth-Century Egypt.* Cambridge: Cambridge University Press, 1985.

Turc, Nicolas. *Chronique d'Egypte: 1798–1804.* Trans. Gaston Wiet. Cairo: Institut Français d'Archéologie Orientale, 1950.

Walz, Terry. *Trade between Egypt and Bilad al-Sudan.* Cairo: Institut Français d'Archéologie Orientale du Caire, 1978.

INDEX

waqf, also *waqfiyya* (pl. *waqfiyyat* or
   awqaf), 2, 3, 4, 14, 36, 51, 53, 60,
   72, 73, 74, 77, 86, 88, 116, 123,
   125, 136, 141, 155–156, 157, 159,
   160
wikala, 21, 40, 57, 60, 62, 66, 72,
   79, 80, 92, 93, 94, 95, 144, 145
wives. *See* marriage

Zubaida, 12, 79

9 780292 717367